Telling Pieces

• • • • • • • • • • • • •

Art as Literacy in Middle School Classes

Telling Pieces

•••••••••••••

Art as Literacy in Middle School Classes

Peggy Albers
Georgia State University

Sharon Murphy
York University

LEA

LAWRENCE ERLBAUM ASSOCIATES, PUBLISHERS

2000   Mahwah, New Jersey   London

Lawrence Erlbaum Associates, Inc., Publishers
10 Industrial Avenue
Mahwah, NJ 07430

Cover design by Kathryn Houghtaling Lacey

Library of Congress Cataloging-in-Publication Data

Albers, Peggy.
    Telling pieces: art as literacy in middle school classes/ Peggy Albers, Sharon Murphy.
        p.   cm.
    Includes bibliographical references and index.
    ISBN 0-8058-3463-X (paperback: alk. paper)
        1.   Art—Study and teaching (Middle school)—United States. 2. Art in education—United
    States.   I. Murphy, Sharon, 1955-   II. Title.

    N362.5. A43   2000
    707'.1'273--dc21   99-046208
                                                                 CIP

The final camera copy for this work was prepared by the author, and therefore the
publisher takes no responsibility for consistency or correctness of typographical style.
However, this arrangement helps to make publication of this kind of scholarship possible.

Books published by Lawrence Erlbaum Associates are printed on
acid-free paper, and their bindings are chosen for strength and durability.

Printed in the United States of America

10 9 8 7 6 5 4 3 2 1

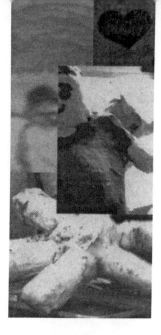

CONTENTS

PREFACE

> Openings are already directed toward closings. The first question in presenting a body of work is where to cut in.
> —Young (1987, p. viii)

Our opening is a reflection on how the questions that form the central part of the book made us think about the practice of artistic representation in our own lives and the insights that our study of sixth-grade art representations might help us make into our own experience. As we were working on the last stages of writing this book, we both were enrolled as novices in hand-building pottery classes. Peggy already had completed one semester of wheel pottery in a studio setting run by professional potters and was going on to complete the hand-building course in the same locale. Sharon enrolled in a class run by a hobbiest potter, who taught occasionally at the local community center. Sharon's class was located in a general arts and crafts room bordered by a gymnasium on one side and general classrooms on the other, where the air was punctuated by the odor of chlorine from the swimming pool down the hall.

Peggy continues in pottery and Sharon does not. We have had numerous discussions about why this might be so. Was it the studio atmosphere, the bountifulness of materials, and the expectation for productivity in Peggy's setting that enabled her to go forward? Was Sharon's interest discouraged by the step-by-step lessons in which the whole group had to wait for the teacher to show the next step, clay was meted out in tiny portions so that it took on a high value, and only some elements of the process were visible (e.g., only certain glazes were available and firing was done by someone the students never met)? Was it simply the congeniality of the physical space? Was it that Peggy might have been more passionate about the medium at the outset? Were other circumstances in our lives factors? We speculate.

Our speculation continues to be informed by the focus of this book: our systematic study of how preadolescent middle school children develop a knowledge and understanding of the conventions of art, what we call *literacy in art*, and how they use their knowledge of conventions to create representations of their lives in a small U.S. town.

In *chapter* 1, we introduce the book, using a quotation from Jeanette Winterson (1995) to develop the concept of *art as literacy*. The remainder of the chapter sketches the theoretical framing for the text and the relation of the chapters to each other.

Chapter 2 presents the principles of social semiotic theory as a lens through which to consider how meaning is represented, whether in print or visually. The following six principles are presented:

1. Meaning is represented through the use of semiotic systems
2. Semiotic systems can be of different types (e.g., visual, social, cultural)
3. Any instance of a semiotic system in use creates a "text"
4. Within any single text, semiotic systems may overlap, co-occur, and work with or against the meanings of the other system(s)
5. Within semiotic theory, literacy is facility in the process of creating or interpreting the signs of one or more semiotic systems used by the larger social collective
6. Texts are inherently ideological.

The chapter then moves from this theoretical framework to consider how research on emergent literacy is informed by semiotic theory and can, in turn, inform an understanding of visual literacy. The following key issues are discussed:

1. The role of intentionality in the representation of meaning
2. When representations are considered sufficient and complete
3. The significance of experimentation and hypothesis testing in representing meanings
4. How repetition of semiotic elements creates a pool from which many meanings can be generated

5. The nature of how representations display information about the meanings represented
6. How prior representational forms and meanings are revisited throughout the artistic life span
7. The way in which conventions relating to the representation of meanings can be both liberating and constraining
8. The way in which all texts created reflect ideological positioning.

Chapter 3 presents a sampling of the artworks collected for the study, some of which are discussed in later chapters. The presentation of the students' artworks in a galleria offers viewers and readers the opportunity to interpret the works independently from our interpretations of them. It also is an effort to disclose the students' works in a presentational style that treats them in a manner similar to the way in which adult artworks are treated. In essence, the chapter stands as a challenge to the positioning of children's artworks as somehow less important than other artworks, even though art historians and interpretivists such as Fineberg (1997) have demonstrated not only that many modern artists held extensive collections of children's art, but that they drew significantly from these collections, sometimes mimicking them.

Chapter 4 explores three themes in relation to the focus of the study. The first, a study of location, presents not only a description of the research context but sets out possible influences on the young artists who participated in the study. Of particular note in relating this tale of location are the dominance of evangelical Christian religion and the undercurrents of racism and homophobia that have rippled through the community. We also present information on the sixth-grade art class as a location that represents difference in announced and unannounced ways: announced through the way in which the art curriculum is represented officially and unannounced in the assumptions that undergird perceptions of the art class and the teaching practices of others in the school. Following this discussion are the tales of loss and longing that students reveal in relation to their senses of themselves as artists and the kinds of artistic engagements they long to have. Through interview and journal data, the students reveal, in their own words, their history with art both as a process and a body of knowledge. This history hints at imagined and real losses of a passion for art, the diminishment of emergent literacy skills in art because of immersion in limiting environments, and the push and pull of peer culture on the artistic sensibilities of these young adolescents.

Chapter 5 focuses on how one teacher of the sixth-grade art class created a pedagogical situation wherein her emphasis on freedom, form, and feedback created opportunities for students to satiate some of their longings in relation to art as literacy. We describe how the art teacher expected that, after a demonstration of a practice, technique, or skill, students would take up the freedom to explore the practice, technique, or skill in whatever way they wished. Through excerpts from classroom interactions and teacher interviews, we describe how the teacher recognized that immersion in visual culture was not enough for students: These emerging artists had to have their attention drawn to techniques and skills, but the art teacher also recognized that the students could learn to control and elaborate on techniques and skills only if they were given the opportunity to work on self-inspired artistic representations, and that optimal learning occurred when feedback was provided in the context of the production of these representations. We conclude that although students generated works in the traditional media characteristic of their early elementary school experiences with art, the range of media they used indicated the power of the combined demonstrations, opportunities, and pedagogical interventions that heightened students' attentiveness to skills and techniques in the process of creating a representation.

In *chapter* 6, we consider how the artworks created by the students represented meaning, and how student identities and community ideology permeated these meanings. Through interview excerpts and observational notes, the students present, in their own words, the grounds for our interpretation of their artworks—artworks filled with images of racial hatred and gender stereotyping.

In the concluding chapter, *chapter* 7, we argue for the importance of art as a significant part of the curriculum. We consider the tensions inherent in arguments for teachers to be artist educators, the arguments for and against Discipline–Based Art Education (DBAE), and the current climate for enlarging art education in schools. Curricular frameworks such as those in Italy and England are considered as starting points for development. However, we do not stop our discussion at art as literacy, but raise questions about how to work with textual representations, even when those representations are offensive. We consider how a participatory-centered pedagogy that works toward the goal of human freedom and dignity might look because such a pedagogy would enable any classroom (Simon, 1992), not just the classroom working with artistic representations.

Acknowledgments

We acknowledge our appreciation of the participants in the study, in particular the teacher, Louise Woolf, who, ironically, remains closeted through the regulatory framework of research confidentiality, but whose story is a lesson to all who read it. In addition, we want to thank Naomi Silverman, who was willing to take a chance on a book that traversed traditional disciplinary lines, and the reviewers of our book, who provided us with positive comments that spurred on our momentum. Linda Eisenberg also provided invaluable assistance in the last stages of text production. Finally, we want to thank Susan Murphy, whose assistance on last-minute typing and reference checking allowed us to meet our production schedule.

—Peggy Albers
—Sharon Murphy

INTRODUCTION

In her essay, "Art Objects," Jeanette Winterson (1995) spoke of walking past the window of a little art gallery in Amsterdam . . .

> . . . and in the moment of passing [I] saw a painting that had more power to stop me than I had power to walk on.
>
> The quality of the draughtsmanship, the brush strokes in thin oils, had a Renaissance beauty, but the fearful and compelling thing about the picture was its modernity. Here was a figure without a context, in its own context, a haunted woman in blue robes pulling a huge moon face through a subterranean waterway. (p. 3)

Winterson's (1995) reverie around a particular moment of viewing a piece of art is a reminder of the multiple levels through which works of art can tell tales—tales of what art is thought to be, tales of the craft of art, tales of culture, tales of the participants in the culture, tales of what is valued and what is not. This book is an excavation of some possible tales art tells. By reflecting on the activities of sixth graders at work in an art class, we examine the tales these young representatives and their artworks tell of the literacy practices in one instance of educational and social life.

We frame this book by linking literacy and art.[1] We use the phrase *literacy in art* quite broadly to denote knowledge about art. By knowledge about art we mean the collection of practices, or the field of sociohistorical knowledge associated with the field of art, or both. Knowledge about line, form, space, composition, technique, and media exemplifies what constitutes literacy in the practices of art. This kind of knowledge was gestured

1

to by Winterson (1995) when she spoke of media and technique in the phrase, "the brush strokes in thin oils" (p. 3). Winterson also signaled the sociohistorical element in art when she referred to "a Renaissance beauty" (p. 3). Her reference recalls a significant cultural period and the representational forms associated with that period. Knowledge of the sociohistorical aspect may include knowledge of social movements and art's place within them.

As part of our exploration of literacy, we also consider in art the artist's representation of a particular content while working within the practices and sociohistorical traditions of visual representation, and the interpretation of the artist's representation by readers/viewers. In essence, then, the representational power of any artwork/text (whether that literacy is visual or linguistic) lies in the meaning potential of the artwork/text for readers/viewers (Halliday, 1978).[2] Winterson (1995), for instance, noted the image of the painting that stopped her: "a figure without a context, in its own context, a haunted woman in blue robes pulling a huge moon face through a subterranean waterway" (p. 3). In this phrase, Winterson showed that she was struck not just by the haunting image rendered by the artist, but by the double moment of the "timeboundedness" of the figure represented and the modernity of a piece that clearly was created long before Winterson's interpretive encounter.

Representing Meaning

We begin our exploration of art as literacy in chapter 2 by considering what it means to represent meaning. The representation of meaning in a variety of forms is an inherently human act. Writing, visual art, and music are among the forms that immediately come to mind as the kinds of efforts humans make toward expressing meanings for others to interpret (Langer, 1957). In exploring how representation works, we draw on concepts used to think about language and use a semiotic framework to guide our thinking.

In our interpretation of semiotic theory, we use a social semiotic perspective (Halliday, 1978; Kress & van Leeuwen, 1996; Moxey, 1994) in which semiotic systems are conceived very broadly to denote any collection of elements used in relation to each other to represent meaning. This definition is a very open one allowing for many possibilities of meaning representation (visual, linguistic, social, and cultural) to be considered within a similar framework. Any single instance of representation, such as a particular artwork or a particular piece of writing created, is a text available for reading and interpretation. In any one text, semiotic systems can overlap and co-occur with other semiotic systems and, in doing so, can work with or against the other systems. For instance, the visual rendering of a word may be the opposite of the word's linguistic meaning.

Literacy in a semiotic system is facility in the process of creating or interpreting the signs of one or more semiotic systems used by a social collective. This conceptualization of literacy fits well with how we are thinking about literacy in art: Knowledge about the collection of practices and sociohistorical knowledge associated with the field of art is knowledge concerning the creation and interpretation of the semiotic systems used in art. The openness of semiotic theory enables us to stretch the conceptualization of literacy by drawing on the idea that signs work within a social collective and, as a consequence, are inherently ideological. Volosinov (1983) suggested that "the sign is a creation between individuals, a creation within a social milieu . . . Only that which has acquired social value can enter the world of ideology, take shape and establish itself there" (p. 22). Semiotic theory extends the definition of literacy so that the sociohistorical practices and knowledge associated with art can be considered in terms of power relations and social values.

With this framing in place, we explore the ontogenesis of written literate practices for very young children. The power of this exploration for visual art lies in the fact that recent research in the field of emergent literacy (Ferreiro & Teberosky, 1982; Harste, Woodward, & Burke, 1984; Steward, 1995) reveals children's progressions and regressions as they move toward conventionality in written language representation. These intellectual moves are invariably intertwined with children's efforts to disambiguate written language from visual art in terms of both form and function. This research stands in contrast to, but yet complements, the research into developmental theories about children's learning of art (Bland, 1968; Brittain, 1979; Hildredth, 1941; Lindstrom, 1957; Lowenfeld & Brittain, 1982; Paine, 1981) and the romantic vision of children's work as revealing an innocent eye (Fineberg, 1997). In essence, these bodies of research converge on the fact that the opportunity to become literate in art is a function of the opportunities each individual has with art, and these, in turn, are often related to the social value placed on art.

The Study

We begin our exploration of one art teacher's classes in Riverview Middle School (RMS) located in a large U.S. town.[3] We open our exploration in chapter 3 with a presentation of the pieces generated by the students in the class. We present their work in the form of a galleria–a show that takes the artworks out of the context of the events in the classroom and places them in a visual space, where the possibilities for interpretation are open to reactions such as Winterson's (1995), where our interpretations as researchers do not intrude on the works and do not begin to direct the possibilities of interpretation (Paley, 1995). We realize that the reproduction of the artworks in black-and-white as well as the photographic reproduction already layers an interpretive film over the pieces. Nevertheless, we believe that the opportunity for the reader/viewer to interpret the pieces independently of any critical text allows the pieces to tell their own tales for each reader/viewer, creating multiple moments of interpretive possibility, not unlike those Winterson noted earlier.

If the pieces are viewed before the reading of our interpretive text is undertaken, we think that readers/viewers may enjoy moments of surprise, dismay, disagreement, tolerance, or recognition in relation to the interpretations we have brought to bear on the images presented. In addition, the presentation of the artworks in this formalistic way implicitly troubles the assumption of "whether children and youth have anything to contribute to a society's cultural capital" (Paley, 1995, p. 3). In essence, it asks why children's art is largely forgotten, ignored, or suppressed by cultural institutions and challenges the viewer to consider what such forgetting, ignorance, and suppression might mean.

Our interpretation begins in chapter 4 with the work of the principal researcher in this project, Peggy Albers. Drawing on archival data and contemporary sources, Peggy creates a picture of the context in which the work was created, the town of Riverview: a town covering the range of socioeconomic status, but in which 95% of the population is White; a town wherein evangelical Christian religion is dominant; a town with an active Ku Klux Klan (KKK). Across a period of 2 years, Peggy observed and collected data on more than 400 students who passed through one art teacher's classes. Using the interviews, artworks, journals, school documents, classroom handouts, and field notes that Peggy collected as a starting point, we examine how the sixth graders in the classes she observed grew toward literacy in art; the ways in which they represented the ideas, feelings, and culture that permeated their existence; and some of the interpretations that arise in relation to their artworks.

Six to 9 weeks[4] is not a long time to make an impact on the lives of students. Yet, this is the range of time that Louise Woolf, the art teacher at RMS, had to work with each of her classes. We begin our exploration of the students' learning by revealing, in their own words, their history with art as a process and as a body of knowledge. This history hints at imagined and real losses of a passion for art, the diminishing of emergent literacy skills in art because of immersion in limiting environments, and the push and pull of peer culture on the artistic sensibilities of these young adolescents.

In the context of Louise Woolf's literate art classroom, sixth graders encountered several features that distinguished it from many of their school-based art experiences of the past. To begin with, Louise maintained an expectancy that students would view art class in a manner not unlike that of the studio art classes characteristic of her own art education, wherein an aspect of artistic practice, technique, or skill was demonstrated and students then were provided with the opportunity to explore that practice, technique, or skill in whatever way they wished. In addition, she recognized that immersion in visual culture was not enough for students. These emerging artists had to have their attention drawn to techniques and skills. However, Louise also recognized that the students could learn to control and elaborate on techniques and skills only if they were given the opportunity to create self-inspired artistic representations. These opportunities included not only freedom of choice for the content and direction of a piece, but typically also a choice in the media that could be used and allowance for collaborative efforts in the production of artworks. Although Louise's students generated works in the traditional media characteristic of their early elementary school experiences with art, the range of media they used in her class was an indication of the power of the combined demonstrations, opportunities, and pedagogical interventions that heightened students' attentiveness to skills and techniques in the process of creating a representation.

We interpret the creations of Louise's students in several ways. In chapter 5, we first of all consider these representations as artifacts of social history, a social history that carries with it concepts of sexuality, gender, race, class, and other identities. Two principal routes are used to carry out this exploration. One route is through the actions and talk of the students during the creation of artworks. The second route follows a series of interviews conducted by Peggy and Louise with the students in the class. These interviews ask the students to respond to questions about palette choices in artistic representations and the content of what is represented. Together, these opportunities provide a grounding for a contextualized interpretation of the artworks generated, an interpretation that remembers the contexts (classroom, school, and community) surrounding the production of the artworks, speculating on how these contexts inform students' representational efforts.

Indeed, it is toward the creation of artistic representational and interpretive possibilities that we turn for our concluding chapter. In this chapter we argue, as Kress and van Leeuwen (1996), Laspina (1998), and many others have insisted, that the visual world needs much more consideration in educational circles. However, our arguments are about the kinds of conditions that make it possible for children and adults to explore art. We consider, for example, the dilemma of the generalist teacher who personally may be uneducated in art. We consider the arguments for and against Discipline–Based Art Education. Also, we consider the current sociopolitical climate for enlarging art education in schools.

With that framework in place, we lay out what we believe are directions for pedagogical possibilities in art education. In our framework, we consider how opportunities for literacy in art can be enabled. Here we draw on curricular frameworks from Britain, the United States, and Italy as a starting point for development. In addition, we ask ourselves and others to think about the responsibilities of literacy: We raise questions about how to work with artist's representations, even when those representations are offensive. We raise questions about how to trouble simplistic interpretive frameworks, and, we raise questions about how to do all of this while considering the artist's representational desires. In short, we are raising the possibility of creating a kind of education that is neither child centered nor teacher centered. Instead, it is participatory centered (Murphy, 1995). It is, as Simon (1992) called it, a "pedagogy of possibility, one that works for the reconstruction of social imagination in the service of human freedom" (p. 4).

NOTES

1   Throughout this textbook we use the term *art* to denote the visual arts. We recognize that the term *art* can be used to refer to a spectrum (e.g., literature, music, visual arts). Our use in this textbook is for convenience.

2   We model the idea of meaning potential after the work of Halliday (1978), whose work was applied recently to visual representation by Kress and van Leeuwen (1996).

3   For details on research methods, please see the appendix.

4   In the first year of the study, classes were held in 6 week blocks. In the second year of the study, they were in 9 week blocks. Much of the data presented is from the second year of the study.

THE REPRESENTATION
OF MEANING

The desire to represent and communicate meaning is a fundamental feature of being human. We are not unique in taking this position. We align
ourselves with a cadre of thinkers from art theoreticians and art educators
(Thompson, 1990; Tickle, 1996a, 1967b) to anthropologists (Hall, 1976)
linguists (Halliday & Hasan, 1989), psychologists and philosophers (e.g.,
Dewey, 1934; Langer, 1957), and literacy educators (e.g., Goodman, 1994;
Harste et al., 1984). Like many of these thinkers, we argue that being human means not only struggling to make sense of our environment and our
place in it, but sharing and elaborating on that struggle with others. Human beings strive to make sense of life. We seem to find solace, challenge,
pleasure, and sociality in representing our sense-making to others and in
considering and interpreting the sense-making of others.[1]

The fact that *language*[2] immediately comes to mind when sense-making is considered reflects its psychical dominance as a representational
form in contemporary society (Hawkes, 1977). However, we want to use
language as a stepping stone for considering other forms of representation, forms such as those in the sixth-grade classroom we present. We
want to explore how concepts and thinking about language can help us
consider how representation works. We follow Kristeva's (in Hawkes, 1977)
claim that "the *major constraint* affecting any social practice lies in the
fact that it signifies; *i.e.* that it is articulated *like* a language" (p. 125). In
doing so, we adopt semiotic theory,[3] a framework that theorizes signification and representation, to help us lay the foundation for linking art and
literacy.

7

Social Semiotics as a Framework

The theory we use to inform our work is social semiotics, drawing on Halliday (1978), Kress and van Leeuwen (1996), and Moxey (1994).[4] The principles we derive from semiotic theorizing are several.

The Representation of Meaning Occurs Through the Use of Semiotic Systems. Semiotic systems involve collections of elements used in relation to other elements to represent meaning. The traffic light is one example of a semiotic system (Carter, Goddard, Reah, Sanger, & Bowering, 1997). Together, in a specific context, the red, amber, and green colors of the traffic light create the system. The meaning of the system does not reside in any one of the lights, but in how the lights are interpreted in relation to each other. For example, in other semiotic systems, the color red can represent joy, robustness, or any number of qualities, but in the semiotic system of the traffic signal, each colored visual display has a particular meaning: green for "proceed," amber for "proceed with caution," and red for "do not proceed." Other color elements are not recognized as part of the system: Blue does not work in the North American system, nor does brown or violet.

A semiotic system is such that only particular combinations or patterns in the system are recognized as being possible. For example, if red and green signals are simultaneously displayed, the interpreters of the display would assume that the system is broken rather than assume new meanings for this combination. Therefore, even when a particular instance of use (which we refer to as a text) appears to violate the rules of the semiotic system, the rules of that system are still used to think about the specific text.

Semiotic Systems Can Be of Different Types: Visual, Social, Cultural and So On. It is possible to imagine many types of semiotic systems and innumerable texts that can be generated in each of these systems. Again, Carter et al. (1997) provided illustrative examples of semiotic systems from which texts emerge.

Visual semiotic systems, for instance, can include representations as diverse as oil on canvas, films, books, sculptures, subway advertisements, magazine articles, and modes of dress. Each of these, in part or whole, uses the visual mode of representation. Take the example of a dress code: Fabrics, colors, and styles are among the elements making up this semiotic system. In the same way that the traffic signal has restrictions of possible colors and combinations, the dress code operates with its set of representational and interpretive conventions. For instance, some fabrics, colors or styles are not worn with others. Many haute couture fashion shows include creations that are sensational because they violate the code. Thus when an actress shows up at a gala event wearing a dress made of credit cards, the sensationalism is, for some, a wonderment at the violation of the code and, for others, a moment for moving forward to revise the code. Consequently, although there is a normativity to the code, the code can change.

In Any Particular Text That Is Created, Semiotic Systems May Overlap, Co-occur, and Work with or Against the Meanings of the Other System(s). Texts may use multiple resources or modes to represent meaning. For instance, the mode used in a telephone conversation is verbal. The text created in the telephone conversation is marked by resources of word choice, intonation, pitch, silence, and sound, along with unseen (and therefore uninterpreted by the telephone listener) gestures. However, if a conversation is written, it changes: Even though word choices might remain the same, ambiguities or alteration in meanings may result because print does not fully capture the intonation of oral conversation, even when maximizing the use of typographic elements such as punctuation, font size, or font style. For example, even though the words in each of the sentences in Fig.1.1 are identical, if the underlined word in each of the sentences is said emphatically, the meaning of the sentence changes.

Written language calls on typographic resources to reduce ambiguity.[5] For example, it can use simple features such as the underlining illustrated in Fig. 1.1, or, as illustrated in Fig. 1.2, it can use font size and style to gesture visually to the amount of emphasis intended. Furthermore, it can use a variety of words to signify how some words are to be read (e.g., angrily, haughtily, solemnly). In essence, then, even though the words of language[6] remain constant, the semiotics of the representational mode (auditory/visual) used along with language have an impact on what is represented and interpreted.

The book is on the table.	
<u>The</u> book is on the table.	The book is <u>on</u> the table.
The <u>book</u> is on the table.	The book is on <u>the</u> table.
The book <u>is</u> on the table.	The book is on the <u>table</u>.

FIG. 1.1 An example showing the effect of emphasis on meaning.

FIG. 1.2 Example showing the use of visual resources in representing sound.

Competing semiotic systems in one representational effort can create interpretive tensions for people when the systems present conflictive information. A classic example of the multisemiotic nature of print and the tension that competing semiotic systems in a text present is illustrated by a psychology experiment known as the Stroop effect. In the experiment, readers are presented with lists of color words, but the ink used to print the words may not be the same color as the word names (e.g., "blue" is printed in yellow ink, "yellow" in red ink, and so on). Across several decades of study, researchers consistently demonstrate that when the visual and the linguistic semiotic systems are in conflict, readers take slightly more time to read words than when the visual and linguistic semiotic systems are operating synchronously (Rayner & Posnansky, 1978; Stroop, 1935). The readers' hesitancy suggests that the conflictive information makes them pause ever so slightly to make a choice about semiotic priorities in relation to the task.

Literacy Is Facility in the Process of Creating or Interpreting the Signs of One or More Semiotic Systems Used in Agreed-on Ways in a Social Collective. Each of the elements in a semiotic system is a sign. In a painting or sculpture, among the signs with which the painter works are form, line, shape, composition, space, and color. In a written text, the signs with which the writer works are graphic letters and characters, their presentation on the page, and the words of language.

In essence, then, the common foundational base of print and art literacy is that they are representational creations or signs (Bloome & Bailey, 1992; Goodman, 1994; Kress & van Leeuwen, 1996; Moxey, 1994). These signs are saturated with sociocultural history. In working with representational elements (whether clumsily, adeptly, or adroitly), artists and writers demonstrate one aspect of literacy: the process of using (and sometimes extending) the conventions of a semiotic system, at a particular moment in time, to represent meanings.

Two examples, one from art and one from written language, illustrate the fact that we may not even be aware of the conventions that guide our current use of signs. Our first example comes from the way line is used to represent movement in drawings. As illustrated in Fig. 1.3, curving lines placed around a rounded object are used to indicate that the image is spinning.

FIG. 1.3 Example of a cultural convention in art.

However, as Hubbard (1989) reported, viewers of similar images in some non-Western cultures do not interpret the curving lines as indicative of motion. In fact, they are bemused by this convention. Yet, to members of Western culture, the meaning of this convention is so transparent that they may not even recognize it as a convention.

Written texts are replete with similar examples. For instance, during the time of the ancient Romans, the alphabet used in texts had only one form: what we now call capital letters. The emergence of "small" or low-ercase letters is attributed to (a) the desire of scribes to write more smoothly and rapidly, (b) the development of smoother surfaces (i.e., parchment and vellum as opposed to papyrus) that enabled more rapid writing, and (c) the influence of cursive writing used for daily transactions (McMurtie, 1989). As this example illustrates, the convention of upper- and lowercase letters has a lengthy history that is not considered by most users of written language today.

Similarly, the language represented in written texts is a carrier of thousands of years of social negotiation. The use of negation in written English provides another example. Multiple negation (e.g., "I never said nothing") in written English was quite common until the mid-17th century. However, after this period, a shift occurred, in part because of the influence of Latin (which prohibited double negation) on English prose writing, and in part to avoid ambiguities that seemed to occur when double negation was used in print (Milroy & Milroy, 1991).

These examples illustrate that literacy includes not only the use of elements in a semiotic system but also the invention of elements in the system. Invention extends the sign system if new signs invented by individuals are adopted by a larger social collective. This does not mean that the movement toward convention is easy. The tension between convention and invention permeates the interpretation of texts as well as the production of them. For instance, one need only look at the newspaper clippings of the time to learn that the paintings of impressionists were decried as art (White, 1978), whereas now impressionist work is so strongly recognized and used in popular culture that impressionist images may be the first to come to mind when art is mentioned.

The interpretation of written texts depends on what a text offers as well as issues such as context (Anderson, 1985), background knowledge (Johnston, 1984; Langer, 1984), and culture (Bartlett, 1932), but these factors alone do not explain the variabilities of interpretation that occur when readers relate their interpretations of texts. The individual's disposition also plays into how texts are interpreted. Our dispositions are revealed very early in our lives. For example, Thomas and Chess's (1977) research illustrates that, from infancy, individuals appear to interact with the world in ways that differ from the ways of their parents. In essence, we are asserting our individuality. This individuality, along with the varied experiences the individual has in the culture and the demands of particular situations, comes into play in the invention and interpretation of elements of semiotic systems. For artists and writers, as well as the readers of their texts, the convention of signs offers the possibility for some degree of shared meaning informed by the individual and the larger social collective.

Texts are Ideological. Because signs are created for use between and among individuals, they have social value. Convention is, after all, one way of assigning value. The adoption of a convention indicates the value that a social collective has for a particular sign and the interpretive practices associated with the sign. Because signs have worth, they reflect the ideology of the social collective adopting them. Ideology is "the taken-for-granted assumptions, beliefs, and value systems which are shared collectively by social groups. And, when the ideology is that of a particularly powerful social group, it is said to be *dominant*" (Simpson, 1993, p. 5).

Some, such as Ferguson (1990), have argued that the dominant ideology is like a phantom center, so permeating society and so powerful that it is not named. Instead, it provides the assumptions under which we all operate. To illustrate, Ferguson (1990) provided the following example:

> When we see that a TV show is called *The History of White People in America* we know at once that the genre is comedy. The history of

America and the history of white people are read as synonymous, so
this program can't be serious. The joke is in the tautology. (p. 11)

In writing and art, the representation of gender provides a common
example of how ideology works. In written texts, and in language in general, the historical use of the male pronoun in referring to all of humanity
(he = humanity) illustrates a male-centered value system (Simpson, 1993).
Such usage naturalized the male as dominant, and effectively rendered the
female invisible. Not until the women's liberation movement was there
widespread societal consideration that such representational issues were
problematic (Lakoff, 1990).

In art, the dominance of the male also is evident. The male gaze characteristic of much Western art is exemplified in Garb's (1993) discussion
of a late 19th-century short story in which a woman artist, in a seeming
turn of events, paints the male nude. Even though the story might seem to
indicate that the traditional male gaze has been broken, Garb's (1993) analysis of the story's twists and turns quickly demonstrated that the story works
to "contain and police female sexuality, reinscribe it as lack, and subordi-
nate it to male desire" (p. 38).

Because texts are constructions of a social collective, they are ideological. Their ideological positions may be represented explicitly and implicitly, revealing the place of power (e.g., class, race, and ethnicity) in
which one's representations are situated.

The semiotic framework outlined is the starting point for our consideration of art and literacy. Semiotic theory provides a series of core principles that relate to the making and interpreting of texts. These principles
lay the groundwork for the next step in our exploration of art as literacy—
the visual artistry of young children.

Emerging Visual Artistry

When a young child's seemingly accidental splash of color on a page is
comparable with that of a contemporary artist's work, has the child created art? Has the child demonstrated literate behavior? When a young
child picks up a familiar text and begins reciting the text verbatim without
attending to the print on the page, is that literate behavior? Or is it art?

The terms art and literacy[7] are highly slippery and contested terms
even in the popular press (O'Harrow, 1995; Steiner, 1995). Although
semiotic theory provides a theoretical way to begin thinking about literacy,
it is offered grounding by research on the development of visual and writ-

ten literacy in young children (Ferreiro & Teberosky, 1982; Goodman, 1990; Harste et al., 1984; Kress, 1997; Pontecorvo, Orsolini, Burge, & Resnick, 1996; Spodek & Saracho, 1993; Steward, 1995; Teale & Sulzby, 1986). Complementing this research is work on the development of artistic convention (Bland, 1968; Brittain, 1979; Hildredth, 1941; Hubbard, 1989; Lindstrom, 1957; Lowenfeld & Brittain, 1982; Paine, 1981).

Sorting Out Signs

Much of the research on art and young children is about their use of pencil or paintbrush and paper and usually emphasizes drawing (Golomb, 1989). Consequently, it should come as no surprise that a considerable portion of that research, at least since the 1970s, is concerned with drawing only as it can be distinguished from writing. In essence, the concern of this research is on how children sort out the semiotic systems that can be created on paper. Part of the reason for the relatively recent focus on this area involves a change in perspective about the capacities of young children.

Experimental and observational research since the late 1960s has demonstrated that the infant is a highly competent and complex individual (Astington, 1993; Bullowa, 1979; Vasta, 1982). What once were assumed to be random behaviors in infants are now regarded by researchers as intentional acts (Bullowa, 1979). At the heart of this realization is an understanding of how children come to discover what the mind is and what it does. As Astington (1993) suggested,

> The mind represents—that's what it does—and the mind is the sum of these mental representations—that's what it is. Thus we can think of *representation* in two ways. "A representation" is a mental state, thought, want, belief, intention, and so on, whereas "representation" (without the indefinite article) is the art of forming these mental states. Representation is thus both an *activity* and an *entity*, both a process and a product. It is the process by which the mind produces representations. (pp. 27–28)

Markings made by young children provide evidence of both the representational processes and products. Once young children are positioned as intentional, even in a very emergent sense, their markings on paper and their interpretations of the markings of others can be ascribed a very different character than that of random scribbles (Brittain, 1979; Lowenfeld & Brittain, 1982). One of the most powerful dramatic demonstrations of intentionality and representation is found in the observational studies that Ferreiro and Teberosky (1982) conducted into literacy before schooling. Instead of working strictly with an age-stage approach in which sets of behaviors are described as being characteristic of a specific age, these researchers argued that the *experiential* background of children significantly contributes to the children's increasingly complex understandings about graphics and print. They position the child as a hypothesis-maker who is working to simultaneously uncover and invent the graphic systems of writing and drawing. The child uncovers the system while figuring out its normativities and conventions. The child invents as he or she tests hypotheses about these normativities and conventions and the degree of departure the normativities and conventions can bear before a hypothesis falls outside the semiotic system.

Ferreiro and Teberosky (1982) observed that, initially, young children produce and respond to markings in relatively undifferentiated ways. In essence, their first markings on paper move toward an understanding of the power in making a mark—of leaving behind a visible residue of a motion and a meaning potentiality. However, as children come to participate in the print and visual worlds, they begin to differentiate between the types of marking that they make for print or drawing. In essence, they are trying to figure out how the semiotic systems work to represent meaning.

The sample presented in Fig. 1.4, which Sharon Murphy gathered from a child 2 years and 10 months of age, illustrates the child's emerging understanding that the visuality of the semiotic systems of print and drawing are different.[8] When this child was asked to draw, she used long sweeping movements, whereas, when she was asked to write, she used tiny defined movements (also depicted in Fig. 1.5, another writing sample that demonstrates the stability of the "writing" form for this child).

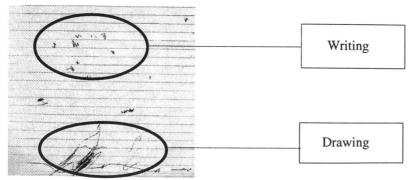

FIG. 1.4 Sample of drawing and writing from a child age 2 years and 10 months.

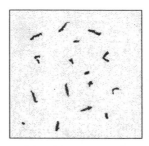

FIG. 1.5 Sample of writing from the same 2-year and 10-month-old child.

Of course, what is missing from Figs. 1.4 and 1.5 for many interpreters of these graphics is the adoption of the normative conventions that
belong to the semiotic systems being used. Consequently, the meaning
potential of these markings is lost in the instant of their making, or it is
available in only limited ways. One way to interpret these markings is to
suggest that what the child has done is produce gross approximations of
the physical actions of others without achieving the same effects. This,
however, gives priority to convention. An alternate interpretation places
these markings at the intersection between convention and invention. That
is, one can imagine that the child has observed the behaviors of others
when they were writing and drawing and has used these observations to
make hypotheses about what writing and drawing entail. These hypotheses became templates for action and the child's markings are the inven-
tions that resulted.

The samples in Figs. 1.4 and 1.5, like samples gathered by researchers
such as Ferreiro and Teberosky (1982) and Harste et al. (1984), indicate
that very young children are beginning to sort out issues related to the
production of representations, apparently realizing that different signs must
be made for each of the semiotic systems involved. For some, such as
Kress (1997), this sorting is much more predisposed toward the picto-
graphic system in that he claimed that "children start [representing the
world] as pictographers" (p. 83). In essence, he argued that they are "drawing print" (Kress, 1997, p. 73).

However, Kress' (1997) interpretation needs to be muted with the understanding that children's sorting out of the characteristics belonging to
the semiotic systems of writing and drawing is quite nuanced. For example, when children are asked to interpret graphic markings, they often
interpret their markings with full realization that adults cannot interpret
them. In the past, this was interpreted as children "playing at" being literate. However, on the basis of Ferreiro and Teberosky's (1982) research,

we now know that this type of interpretive move suggests that young children hypothesize that the meaning potential of signs is available only to the person who makes the signs, rather than to a larger community that has worked out an agreed-on set of conventions. This view probably has a *quid pro quo* kind of sense to it. If children cannot interpret the print markings made by adults, why should adults be able to interpret the markings of children?[9]

Even though the task of sorting out semiotic systems is quite complicated, children appear to do so relatively effortlessly. Rarely, if ever, do we hear of children who have not managed this task, even though we may hear of children who have not attained a specific skill level within one or the other system. Whereas much attention has been focused on moving toward more complex representations in print literacy, the work on moving towards literacy in art pales by comparison.

Literacy in Art: Moving Toward Convention in Art

Interestingly, the move toward convention in art is greeted by a much different response than the move toward convention in print. For instance, Fineberg (1997) gave the following reminder:

> The nineteenth century inherited a double legacy about the child's "innocent eye"; it was innocent enough of convention to see through the emperor's new clothes, so to speak, and at the same time the child was gifted with a privileged view into the mysteries of the divine plan. (p. 5)

Systematic studies of young children's emerging artistry suggest a somewhat less idealized and romanticized view.[10] Indeed, researchers studying young children's development in art represent it as a fairly systematic process. Their interpretations of young children's artworks are often in relation to some imagined idealized photo-realistic image. However, if principles and insights from semiotic theory and studies of emergent print literacy are considered, children's artworks can be viewed in a much different way, not unlike the artworks of their adult counterparts.

Intentionality. The first principle to consider regarding children's artwork involves the *intentionality* of the child's representation (Brittain, 1979; Lowenfeld & Brittain, 1982). Kress (1997) argued that young children's representations start from a point of interest in something they wish to represent. The outcome of a child's interests might result, for example, in the depiction of an automobile as being a pair of round circles because what interests the child about the car is the movement located in the wheels. The wheels stand as a kind of metaphor for the object being depicted. Kress'(1997) interpretation stands in contrast to Hildredth's (1941) interpretation of children's early drawings[11] as "schematic" and "non-pictographic" (p. 63) or Lindstrom's (1957) similar sounding categories[12] of "controlled marks, basic forms, schematic formulae" (p. 18). For Hildredth (1941) and Lindstrom (1957), realistic representation is the barometer of success. For instance, when Hildredth (1941) observes that in the schematic drawings, the child "gets behind the momentary appearance of an object and in his drawing expresses what he knows to be there without regard to realistic appearance; . . . the child infers from what he knows of the object how it should look" (p. 63), her statements imply a lack in the child's representational efforts rather than the possibility that the child may have chosen deliberately to focus on specific elements of interest.

Sufficiency and Completeness. Related to the concept of intentionality are the principles of *sufficiency* and *completeness*, which together signal that the drawing is "enough" to represent what the child artist wishes to represent. Of particular interest here is the child's tendency, regardless of technical accomplishment level, to work with the whole of the representation. Children bring detail into a larger whole so that one sees, for example, the whole structure of the house first, with elements such as windows, chimneys, and so on being added (Hildredth, 1941). As Hildredth (1941) observed:

> The "whole" maintains supreme dominance. . . . The same principle
> is revealed in other phases of child development. The child first be-
> gins to walk and talk "all over." He does not single out some isolated
> psycho-motor skill involved in walking for special practice, nor par-
> ticular words or sounds; instead he works on the problem at the outset
> as a total learning task. . . . Progress in drawing was not made by
> simple addition of juxtaposition, more and more details being added
> to an original detail or two, but by subdivision and differentiation the
> whole was transformed with the addition of new detail and became an
> integrated structure. . . . Differentiation and integration took place
> simultaneously. (pp. 143–145)

Hildredth (1941) speculated that the child's perception of function determines what is included in drawings and concluded that, for the child she studied, details were never omitted because the child thought them to be too difficult to draw. In essence, the child determines what is sufficient to make the drawing complete, and the child's sense of these elements may be quite different from that of the adult.

Experimentation and Hypothesis Testing. The next principle that can be applied to emergent literacy in art would be that of relatively open opportunities for experimentation and hypothesis testing. Bland (1968), for example, like Hildredth (1941) and Lindstrom (1957), reported on the repetitive use of elements in representations, but placed the repetition less within the context of the mastery of realism. In one of the few studies on children's art that extended to media such as clay, Bland (1968) noted that the 3-year-olds she observed "like and need to manipulate materials and to change what they are making as they work. They also take pleasure in doing the same kinds of things over and over" (p. 15). Bland (1968), Brittain (1979), and Lowenfeld (1982) seemed implicitly to position children as being in control of the materials and making choices about how to use them. Such use creates the potential for both convention and invention.

Repetition and Generativity. The child artist working through this early phase of artistic development soon develops what appears to be a repertoire of formulae to use (Bland, 1968; Hildredth, 1941; Lindstrom, 1957). This tendency to use, for instance, a formula that the trunks of trees can be drawn as straight lines, is reminiscent of similar principles described in early print literacy development: (a) the recurring principle in which "the same moves [are] repeated over and over again" (Temple, Temple, & Burris, 1982, p. 29), so that the straight line is always drawn for the tree trunk, and (b) the generative principle in which "a limitless amount of writing can be generated by using a small set of letters, provided they are combined in different ways" (Temple et al., 1982, pp. 29-30), so that using the formula allows the child to draw many different pictures in which one of the elements, the tree trunk, is depicted in a formulaic manner.

Whereas the explanations for repetitive elements that Hildredth (1941) drew upon once again present the child as demonstrating a lack of attentiveness, intentionality, or skill in visual representational work,[13] Lindstrom's (1957) psychological explanation positioned the child as much more deliberate and thoughtful:

> This seems to me to be a manifestation of the well-recognized conservatism and ritualism evident in other fondness for exact repetition of

familiar forms: the exact words of a familiar story, the accented rhythm
of verse of song, or the undeviating order of accustomed acts in the
performance of daily routines. . . . Perhaps the defining of a category
is so pleasing a form of security that it serves as a refuge: the known.
(p. 28)

Predictability and control may well be significant psychological elements
in the child's observable representations. In addition to emotional com-
fort, the predictability and control of repetitive elements in drawings also
may indicate other facets of the child's semiotic activity. For example, in
studies of repetition in conversational discourse, Tannen (1989) reported
that one function of repetition in conversation is to present less dense discourse and, in doing so, to allow a new focus on information. In young
children's artistic activity, an analogous use would be that by drawing sche-
matically, the child can make prominent new, nonschematic information
(drawings, color, placement) in the text. In essence, this would be a very
strategic use of the semiotic system. An alternate interpretation might be
that schematic drawings allow the child to concentrate on other elements
that may or may not be represented. For example, a child may generate a
highly elaborate story for a picture because her or his cognitive resources
are freed up from concentrating on drawing. In this instance, the child
would be focusing on manipulating some aspects of the semiotic system
while holding the others constant. Both of these interpretations are specu-
lative but seem reasonable within the context of the hypothesized intentional child described earlier.

The Display of Informational Competence. As children begin to work with
line and form in their artworks, they also must decide what information to
omit or include in their representations. As noted earlier, interest continues to be an ongoing motivational force (Kress, 1997). Children make
decisions about how to work within the semiotic system to represent the
information they know or notice. In developmental studies of children's
artwork, the stage at which the issue of the informational content of drawings figures most prominently is when the child draws transparently. As
Hildredth (1941) described it, "In attempting to represent objects in space,
children do not draw photographically—the foreparts opaque with respect
to objects behind, suppressing details that are masked in reality. On the
contrary they draw the object as they know it to be" (p. 68). An example of
such a drawing would be one showing the tracks made by an automobile
through the wheels.

More recent work by Hubbard (1989) indicates that children are not naive to the characteristics of their representations. Instead of being unable to create realistic representations, as some researchers claim (Winner, 1982),[14] children who draw transparently seem to work within the constraints of the semiotic system struggling to make decisions about how to represent what they know. Hubbard (1989) provided examples of one child who deliberately let the viewer of the image see what was inside a gift depicted even though, for the receiver of the gift (in the illustration), the gift was a surprise.[15] In essence, the child wanted to let the viewer of the illustration "in on" the perspective of the giver of the gift. Similarly, Hubbard (1989) observed that "children seem to take the realistic view that they will do whatever is necessary for their particular visual purpose" (p. 79).[16] In summary, then, it appears that children are learning the limitations of the semiotic system and its relationship to readers/viewers of their work as well as the normativities that bound it for them at this point in their artistic literacy practices.

Recursiveness. Related to the principles of intentionality, experimentation, and repetition, is the principle of recursiveness. *Recursiveness* refers to the continued exploration throughout the life span of specific themes and techniques. For instance, as Paine's (1981) study on the work of Gerard Hoffning revealed, some of the themes that appeared in his work at 5 and 6 years of age reappeared throughout childhood and adolescence. Paine (1981) observed:

> Progression in drawing was . . . anything but linear, techniques which were mastered at one point seemed to have been forgotten or ignored at a later date and old ideas constantly revisited and refurbished. The struggle to find a personal style began early too . . . only to be lost in a welter of adopted stylisms which finally gave way to the rediscovery of a personal mode. (p. 4)

Hildredth (1941) commented on recursiveness in relation to perspective, observing that it appeared in the drawings of her subject, was lost, and then reappeared again. The principle of recursiveness suggests that developmental theories of children's artworks need to account for such patterns[17] and that such patterns appear to play important roles in the child's emerging control of the conventions of the semiotic system.

Convention as Liberating and Constraining. Increasingly, with time and experience, young artists adopt more and more of the visual representational conventions of society (e.g., three dimensionality, perspective, movement; Hildredth, 1941; Hubbard, 1989). Yet, while learning the conventions of visual representation can be liberating (in that it frees up the child artist from the burden of inventing the visual representative system and allows for generativity and repetition in the creation of many different texts), convention is also constraining. For young children, convention seems to constrain in two ways that are related to each other. First, the normativity signified by conventionality explicitly teaches children that the sign system works in specific ways. Some ways are recognized as valuable and others are not. As noted earlier, children seem to receive a message that what is valued is a realistic rather than an interpretive rendering. As a consequence, children either express a desire to learn a technique and are dissatisfied with the representational modes they control (Lindstrom, 1957) or they abandon art as a productive representational form.

Ideological Positioning. Like the artworks of adults, children's artworks are full of ideological positionings. Assumptions about material wealth, relationships, and theories of power infuse their representations. Much analysis of children's artworks has been done from a psychodevelopmental perspective (Goodenough, 1926; Kellogg & O'Dell, 1967) rather than a sociological one. Studies such as those of Lindstrom (1957), which consider the stereotypical representations of gender in the artworks of 8- to 12-year-old boys and girls, are illustrative of the ways in which systematic study of power relations in children's art reflects the hegemony of the world they are interpreting. The glamorous faces of girls and the rough-and-tumble boys depicted in the artworks of Lindstrom (1957) mirror the society in which the children find themselves. Similarly, Golomb's (1992) investigation into the universalities of graphic development in young children suggests that culture (and, by default, the ideological positionings within the culture) plays a significant part in the narrative themes explored in the artworks of children.

Clearly, for children and adults, the push to represent meaning is an intricate part of life. Yet, it is often the case that as children move into their preadolescent years, their interest in the creation of visual representations diminishes even though they are immersed in a world where visual representation is steadily increasing. In the remaining chapters of this volume, we examine how the experiences of some preadolescents lead to their conceptions about their own creativity and claim on artistic representation and interpretation.

NOTES

[1] We recognize the place the unconscious may have in sign-making, but for the purposes of this project, we are not discussing aspects of the unconscious in sign-making.

[2] We are using the term *language* to denote words. We realize that it is possible to talk, for instance, about the language of art and the grammar of visual design (Kress & Van Leeuwen, 1996), but we are restricting our use of the term *language* for the purposes of this study.

[3] North American literature tends to use the term *semiotics* because it draws on the work of Charles Pierce, whereas the European literature uses *semiology*, the term coined by Saussure (Hawkes, 1977).

[4] The field of semiotics has been influenced by several major scholars such as Pierce, Barthes, Todorov, and Saussure, among others. For an introduction to aspects of this work, please see Hawkes (1977).

[5] Typographers consider many additional features such as the kind of ink, the choice of paper, the distances between letters and words, the line length, the space between lines, the width of margins and so on. They consider each of these elements "as part of an overall judgment about the 'weight', 'colour', or 'atmosphere', of the page as a whole" (Crystal, 1987, p. 190).

[6] Here we are using language somewhat restrictively in an effort to demonstrate that visual and sound semiotic systems also have an impact on language. In reality, of course, language does not operate without either of these systems.

[7] Literacy in contemporary usage refers to knowledge (e.g., computer literacy), and the term *art* has a similar legacy. According to Cohen and Gainer (1995), "The word art derives from the Latin root *ars* which means a special skill or competence that is learned rather than instinctive. In early China the word for art, *yi-shu*, similarly meant any learned skill. During the Middle Ages in Europe all scholarly pursuits, including mathematics, rhetoric, and the attainment of literacy, were included among the arts" (p. 17).

[8] Without the observational notes accompanying these samples, they would be taken for random scribbling, and the important distinction that the child is beginning to make would be lost.

[9] The multisemiotic nature of print complicates matters even further because the boundaries of drawing and print are not always distinctive.

[10] Part of what may be at stake here is the whole issue of what is valued as art. For instance, as Fineberg (1997) pointed out, the work of many modernists was influenced by children's drawings. Yet, the question could be raised as to why children's drawings themselves are not considered art. As Wolff (1993) argued:

> The social history of art shows, first, that it is accidental that certain types of artefact are constituted *as* "art"(purely for non-functional purposes, and as distinct, say, from crafts). Secondly, it forces us to question distinctions traditionally made between art and non-art (popular culture, mass culture, kitsch, crafts, and so on), for it is clear that there is nothing in the nature of the work or the activity which distinguishes it from other work and activities with which it may have a good deal in common. (p. 14)

Even in Wolff's (1993) conceptualization, the absence of a comment upon children's art is notice-able. This is either because she categorizes children's art as art and therefore does not need a category or because she so dismisses children's art that she does not even recognize its absence from consider-ation.

[11]   Hildredth's (1941) work is based on intensive study of a single child. Hildredth drew from a catalog of more than 4000 drawings for her insights.

[12]   Lindstrom (1957) observed 2- to 12-year-olds enrolled in museum art classes.

[13]   For example, Hildredth (1941) used the following descriptive language of these elements: "su-perficial observation . . . imperfectly organized concept" (p. 64).

[14]   Here we are not claiming that children have the same technical sophistication as an adult artist. Rather, we are suggesting that what is interpreted sometimes as technical inability is, instead, the result of intentional decisions made by the child artist.

[15]   Hubbard's (1989) observations lead to a recurring question with respect to the adult interpreta-tion of children's artworks: Why is it that the same techniques valued in modern art (e.g., see Chagal's Pregnant Woman as an example of transparency) are dismissed in children's artworks as demonstra-tive of inadequacy? Once again, it seems that adults interpret children's artworks only in relation to a photo realistic ideal but hold out a different standard for adult artworks. This practice becomes par-ticularly condemnatory when one realizes that many contemporary artists collected children's art-works and used them as the basis for many of their works. It would seem that, in contemporary society, the sanctioning of this interpretive stance can be seen as opportunistic.

[16]   Another example of this is children's strategies in the depiction of movement through time. Hubbard (1989) provided examples of several different strategies used by children. One, for instance, shows someone diving off a diving board, and in the single illustration the person is depicted standing on the board, heading down toward the water, and entering the water. This technique, which departs from the photo realism that seems to be demanded of children as artists, has been used at several points throughout the history of art in Western civilization and is referred to as continuous narrative.

[17]   Such patterns are common in many other areas of learning. For example, in the learning of irregu-lar verb forms, it is common for the correct verb form to appear in a child's speech (e.g., "I ran"), followed by the abandonment of the form (e.g., "I runned"), in which the child overgeneralizes the rule for the creation of past tense verbs, followed by the emergence of the correct form (Lindfors, 1980). Once an intentional and active child learner is theorized, the explanation required for child behaviors becomes much more complex and much less obvious.

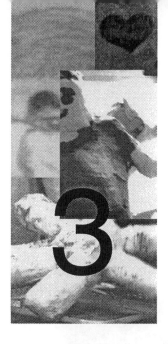

3 GALLERIA

FIG. 3.1 Wire sculpture

FIG. 3.2 Papier mâché sculpture

FIG. 3.3 Work in progress:
Mixed media on paper

FIG. 3.4 Mixed media on paper

25

FIG. 3.5 Graphite on paper

FIG. 3.6 Work in progress:
Papier mâché sculpture

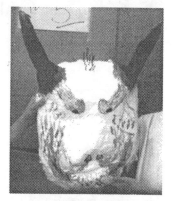

FIG. 3.7 Papier mâché sculpture

FIG. 3.9 Wire sculpture in use

FIG. 3.8 Wire sculpture

FIG. 3.10 Work in progress:
Papier mâché sculpture

FIG. 3.11 Papier mâché sculpture

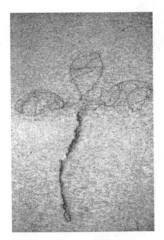

FIG. 3.12 Wire sculpture

FIG. 3.13 Graphite on paper

FIG. 3.14 Acrylic on paper

FIG. 3.15 Work in progress:
Papier mâché sculpture

FIG. 3.16 Work in progress:
Papier mâché sculpture

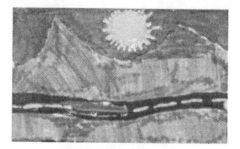

FIG. 3.17 Mixed media

FIG. 3.18 Colored pencil on paper

FIG. 3.19 Mixed media

FIG. 3.20 Colored pencil on paper

FIG. 3.21 Papier mâché sculpture   FIG. 3.22 Graphite on paper

FIG. 3.23 Work in progress: Clay sculpture

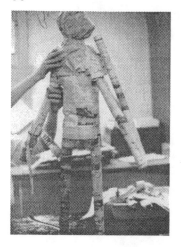

FIG. 3.25 Crayon on paper

FIG. 3.24 Work in progress:
Papier mâché sculpture

FIG. 3.26 Colored pencil on paper

FIG. 3.27 Mixed media on paper

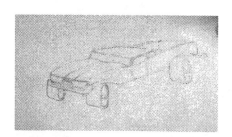

FIG. 3.28 Graphite on paper

FIG. 3.29 Papier mâché sculpture

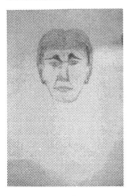

FIG. 3.30 Graphite
on paper

FIG. 3.31 Papier mâché
sculpture

FIG. 3.32 Papier mâché
sculpture

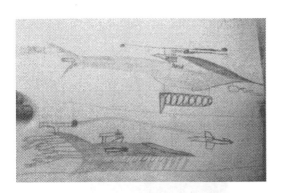

FIG. 3.33 Graphite on paper

FIG. 3.34 Work in
progress: Clay
sculpture

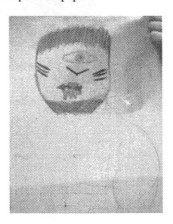

FIG. 3.35 Mixed media on paper

FIG. 3.36 Wire sculpture

FIG. 3.37 Work in progress:
Papier mâché sculpture

FIG. 3.38 Papier mâché sculpture

FIG. 3.39. Clay sculpture

FIG. 3.40 Pastel on paper

4

LOCATION, LOSS, AND LONGING

The distinction between external and internal reality is basic yet vague. Internal reality is not just the reality of the wish, it is also the reality of the body as a place of need. External reality is also not so simple.
—Green (1986, p. 101)

The artworks presented in chapter 3 are representations of ideas, imaginings, wants, and desires. They are a bridge between external and internal realities that begs for contextualization from the larger social space of the lives of these students and the internal realities one might imagine as a consequence. In essence, the semiotics of these artworks asks to be located physically and psychologically so that their meaning potentials can be enriched and extended.

Remembering Britzman's (1998) claim that "while the body must secure its boundaries, it can only do so through attachment" (p. 6), we recognize that external and internal realities are inevitably linked by the ways in which each individual attaches meaning to external realities.

We realize that we can never represent the fulsomeness of the realities experienced by any one person, and that individuals themselves may have difficulty warranting their own senses of themselves. Nevertheless, we try to provide some sense of the possible and articulated attachments that may have contributed to the artistic representations of the sixth-grade students in Ms. Woolf's classes.

Hardworking Days, Racist Nights,
and the Word of God

We begin our tales of location by considering the town of Riverview, the community in which the sixth graders of this study attended school. Located in the state of Riverdale, Riverview is nestled among rolling hills. The town was created by an act of the legislature in the early 1800s, establishing it as the capital city of Riverview County.[1] Early industry in this area developed along resource-based lines: sawmills, a broom factory, marble works, a canning factory, and grain elevators. Riverview continues its agricultural orientation today and is home for many blue collar workers.

Yet with its proximity to a large metropolitan city, more and more white collar workers are moving to this community. With a population of 13,000, Riverview thrives from the 50,000 people who do business in its community. As the county seat, Riverview's growth has been described as "progressive and sure" by its Chamber of Commerce. Superficially, this community resembles many others of its size. It has a Wal-mart, numerous fast food places, and many hotels and restaurants.

Riverview County is home to nearly 60,000 people with a range of socioeconomic backgrounds. Recent census data reveal Riverview County to have a median household income of about $33,000, an unemployment rate of almost 5%, an average wage per job of $18,000, and 7% of the population at the poverty level. Only about 600 of its people are on welfare.

Educational statistics for this county show that nearly 3,000 people have less than a ninth-grade education. A few more than 6,000 residents have no high school diploma, and slightly more than 15,000 have a high school diploma. Approximately 5,000 people in Riverview have an associate, bachelor's, or graduate/professional degree. Riverview and its surrounding area seem to illustrate that hard work and industry provide security, that the economy will provide work for all who are willing and able, and that, apart from a small minority, few have to live in poverty.

The fiscal security experienced by the people of Riverview County is echoed by another type of security, that of knowing exactly who the people of the county are, the security of identity. Of the population in Riverview County, 95% are White, 0.38% are Hispanic, 0.00015% are African American, and the remainder are of other non-White groups. Multiculturalism is not an issue here. Whiteness prevails demographically and psychologically.

For example, although Riverview is said to have had at least one Underground Railway site, which gave aid to slaves in their flight to the North, a little-spoken, yet very well-known belief is that Riverview has little tolerance for non-White ethnic groups and homosexuals. It is generally known that African Americans, especially, are not welcome to live in this town, and that Riverview has an active Ku Klux Klan (KKK) organization. Les, a sixth grader, shared a story concerning the prejudice of this community:

> Everyone here knows that [Riverview] is prejudiced. I have an uncle who is Black, who is married to my aunt and lives in [Pinewood] [a nearby town]. He won't come here because he is afraid so we have to go there. . . . There is a cross [symbol of the KKK] up on the hill near the water tower. They light it up at night so everyone can see it.

Before Les had finished telling his story, Les's partner in art class put his index finger to his lips to silence Les, reminding him that he should not be saying such things. Other students expressed similar beliefs about non-White groups and shared stories of prejudice that lie deep within the "hidden history" of Riverview.

These kinds of words may tell more than the community wishes to reveal. For instance one resident of Riverview comments in a pictorial history of the town that the rumor portraying Riverview as a "community of rednecks and Black haters. . . is BUNK!" and laments that Riverview "has been victimized by a baseless legend [of KKK activity] when other communities have not".[2] Yet, the sharp decline of African Americans in Riverdale is a statistic in need of explanation. One historian of African American heritage in a nearby community speculates that the sharp decline in African American residents in Riverview County may be a result largely of various incidents that have occurred over time in this community: a mob disturbance against a small group of Black immigrants who were invited into the country by the government in an effort to relieve the labor shortage, the slaying of an African American female in the late 1960s, and a murder threat made by a White male against an African American community leader in the 1970s. In addition, efforts of some in the community to counteract racist sentiments remain largely unfulfilled. For example, a group formed in the late 1980s with an antiracist educational agenda was disbanded a couple of years after it was founded.

Race is not the only issue to which the community of Riverview seems to hold in their definition of community identity. Sexual identity is another significant issue. For instance, on two occasions, a large number of parents attended the local school board meetings and expressed their concerns about outcome-based education, hate speech, and intolerance of marginalized groups. The response of the principal was summarized in a newsletter to the faculty of Riverview Middle School (RMS):

> Most of them [the parents] asked good questions, and, in general, I felt the meeting last night was very productive. There were those in attendance who obviously came with an agenda. They were worried about homosexuals, psychological testing, no put-downs, and some other items that seemed to not have much relevance to our corporation. . . . We need to support the efforts our corporation is making. While there are areas that we may think need improvement, there are ways to be heard by working the process. Public education is living in dangerous times. If one of us goes out into the public and talks about the administration or parts of our curriculum in a very disparaging manner, there are those who have agendas against the school who will take those very words we speak and use them against us.

Within this communiqué, the principal alludes to "irrelevant" issues (homosexuality, hate speech, and psychological problems) brought forward by those with "an agenda." Clearly, the principal is confident enough in the community's stance on homosexuality and its acceptance of hate speech to present this portrayal in a public written form.

In seeming contradiction to this portrayal of a racist and homophobic community is the fact that the community of Riverview is home to more than 30 churches representing most major denominations. Yet, a close examination of this "factoid" reveals that Riverview's religious population is predominantly evangelical Christian.[3] Diamond (1990) defined "evangelical" as those who have gone through "born-again conversion" to Christianity and who "believe that the Bible is to be taken literally word for word" (p. 55). Diamond (1990) explained that, at first, evangelism was a "religious phenomenon," but that with the 1976 U.S. presidential election, the political clout of evangelism burgeoned and gained strength in all facets of American life. With Jimmy Carter, Ronald Reagan, and Gerald Ford's self-proclamations as born-again Christians, the 1976 presidential election was the first time since John F. Kennedy's 1960 race that the religious orientation of the candidates was scrutinized (Diamond, 1990). Furthermore, the platform of family values, with its homophobic subtext, has become so much a part of this movement that explicit discussions about the Christian Coalitions' decision about launching a campaign against homosexuality have become the focus of media coverage (Henneberger, 1998).

Given the participation rate in evangelical religion in the community at large, it is no surprise that the evangelical religious influence in RMS is quite prevalent. From the dress of the students, faculty, and personnel to the religious activities in the school, symbols of Christianity abound. For instance, one teacher, in talking with his students, sports a baseball cap on which a red crucifix is embroidered. Middle school students wear jewelry that symbolizes Western religion and clothing with images and words representing their Christian beliefs. One boy wears a T-shirt with a Pepsi-like icon on it: Instead of the word "Pepsi," the word "Jesus" is displayed. These might be generously interpreted as symbols showing the pervasiveness of certain aspects of popular culture, but other elements in the school bear a less generous reading. In the women faculty's rest room, a copy of *The Daily Word*, a monthly religious pamphlet, is placed on a small table directly in front of the toilet. The spine of the pamphlet is firmly pressed open and the daily message/scripture passage highly visible, which seems to encourage a reading of the daily Christian message.

Other instances of religious influence in the school include convocations before school and around the flagpole by some faculty and students, belief in corporal punishment by some faculty as a means to keep students from straying too far from the expected moral behavior, and religious pamphlets, drawings, posters, and proverbs on the walls of several classrooms. Moreover the principal's newsletter to faculty (mentioned above) suggests that "family values" are alive and well at RMS.

Riverview as a location for the emergence of particular sensibilities seems powerful in its singularity—a singularity of economic, racial, sexual, and religious identity. When submersed in such a physical and social location, what space is there left for the teachers and students of Riverview to construct other identities? Is there a need or a desire for such a space?

Riverview Middle School:
A School for "Middle" America

Riverview School District, is responsible for the education of nearly 5,500 students and draws students from several townships. In Riverview, there are three elementary schools, two middle schools, and one high school. The Riverview business community boasts about its high-quality school system, which fashions its courses to fit the needs of students. Ratios of students to teachers at each grade level meet the state requirements and average 18 students per teacher at the elementary, middle, and high school levels. Riverview has a high school graduation rate of 84% and a dropout rate of 16%. The school system places a strong emphasis on academics, yet acknowledges the importance of "nonacademic" activities including band, orchestra, chorus, and drama.

RMS, located in the north part of Riverview, draws a population of students whose home locations range from the wealthiest subdivision lying to the north of Riverview to the most impoverished area near the river. Almost all the students travel to school by bus, bike, or car, with Riverview School District providing transportation for more than two thirds of its students. Riverview School District serves both children from the town and those living in outlying areas, and the demographics of the school reflect this community–country division. Many of the middle/upper class students consider themselves college bound. Although all of the students in this school are of the same racial group, certain speech patterns and accents, dress, school supplies, career aspirations, and interests mark differences among the students. Some are considered "river rats," a euphemism for those living in the poorest area of town.

Riverview Middle School As a Physical Space

The physical layout of RMS is not unlike that of many schools. The single-story building is built from brick, with long hallways and classrooms side by side. At various times throughout the year, the hallway walls are decorated with student work, including posters that illustrate various historical periods, students' favorite heroes, history timelines, and artworks. The RMS classrooms are like many others, often with the desks facing one direction and in straight rows.

According to a Riverview resident who lives across the street from RMS, this middle school is too progressive. She believes that too much liberty is given to students at Riverview. Her impressions of the "modern" changes in RMS are quite negative. She wishes that school would be like it used to be "with the desks firmly positioned on the floor with bolts," and with students more disciplined in their behavior and given less freedom.

Apart from classrooms, other focal points in the school include the main office, gymnasium, multipurpose room, and teachers' lounge. The school's main office is like many others—a large open space with a long counter separating the secretaries from students, faculty, and visitors. The offices of the principal and vice principal are adjacent to the main office. The teachers' mailboxes are open boxes situated in the main part of the office. On the counter there usually are school documents including daily announcements, school policies, and the school calendar of events.

The gymnasium and the multipurpose room are used for athletics as well as for a magazine sale, the talent show, and assemblies in which speakers share their thoughts on social issues directed at adolescents. On one side of the large and spacious gym is a wall of bleachers. During assemblies, students sit according to their age group in specified areas on the bleachers, often with the teacher whose class period they are assigned.

The teachers' lounge resembles many others. The room is decorated in a country style with geese and flower patterns on the wallpaper and furniture. There is a full-size couch, love seat, bookcase, refrigerator, sink, and bulletin board. In the center of the room is a long rectangular table, which serves primarily as the dining table. On the bulletin board are posted notices indicating upcoming events in the school, notices about the legal aspects of school, and "For Sale" notes. The books on the shelves are about various subject area curricula, and largely date back to the early 1970s, yet there are several current periodicals available as resources. Physically, then, RMS is like many other schools. Indeed, on the surface it is the prototypical school of "middle" America—ordered, undistinguished in its physicality, and comfortable in the predictability of its ambiance.

Riverview Middle School as an Organized Pedagogical Space

Riverview Middle School operates with a relatively traditional scheduling system. School classes start at 7:30 a.m. on Tuesday and Thursday, and are delayed on Monday, Wednesday, and Friday for thirty minutes to allow for an advisory/homeroom period. Students who ride the school bus are dismissed at 2:10 p.m., and city students are dismissed 10 minutes later. During the seven periods of 42 minutes each, students are enrolled in year-long "core academic courses" such as English, math, science, social studies, and reading. Enrichment classes, lasting 9 weeks, are also provided. Art, home economics, industrial arts, and QUEST/health are slated as enrichment classes. Many of the teachers at RMS have taught in this system for many years, usually teaching more than one grade level in their subject area. Teachers usually teach five classes with two preparation periods, along with being responsible for other duties including hall monitoring, advising, and teaming with other faculty to integrate subject areas. Others also coach various activities, but these are often paid positions.

The range of pedagogical stances of the teachers at RMS can best be illustrated through two teachers: Ms. Olson and Mr. Carson. One day Ms. Olson, a tall and lanky English teacher, was observed moving smoothly and rapidly down the corridor carrying a wooden paddle with holes in it. Her eyes were focused on what seemed to be her next mission: spanking someone for some wrongdoing. Obedience at all costs seemed to be part of the school's philosophy, and Ms. Olson was a strong proponent of this belief.

On the other hand, the science teacher, Mr. Carson, was a teacher to remember for different reasons. His pursuit of science like the maniacal scientist Christopher Lloyd in the *Back to the Future* films won him favor with students. Outside his classroom door he placed a full-size stand-up cardboard figure of Captain Jean-Luc Picard, starship captain in the *Star Trek: The Next Generation* television series. Always wearing a white laboratory coat adorned with many metal buttons with various expressions imprinted on them, Mr. Carson made sure he warmly greeted his students as they entered his classroom.

Notwithstanding Ms. Olson and Mr. Carson, traditional pedagogical and curricular practices are the norm at RMS. Curricular subject areas are taught in an isolated and unconnected fashion. Mary, a sixth-grade student, talks about her English class in which they "don't do reading. We just have pronouns, adjectives, and stuff like that." Writing "is about different events like we did, like career day, our trip to [Walnut] County and stuff like that." In social studies, students artistically design posters on historical events such as slavery and people including Abraham Lincoln and Frederick Douglass. The content of these posters indicated that students engage little in critical thought about these historical events. Rather, they copy paragraphs and draw or photocopy pictures and photos from their history texts. The information on these posters is very limited and encyclopedic. For instance, one poster centered on the Trail of Tears offended the art teacher, Louise Woolf (who is of Cherokee descent), not because of the subject matter but because the poster lacked any sense of why the Indians were pushed westward. As she said: "I was so offended . . . because it said that the Indians moved to Oklahoma in such and such a year, and it was like, 'Hey, let's just go to Oklahoma.' There was no sense of White repression; it was totally ahistorical."

Teachers lecture to their students. Students take notes on these lectures, and then are tested on these notes. Worksheets are often the fill-in-the-blank, matching, or true–false type, sometimes including design flaws. For instance, in an English worksheet directing students to find the correct sentence in a set of otherwise grammatically incorrect sentences, more than one sentence met the criteria for correctness. In many of the classes, the focus appears to be on mechanical operations, recitation, and memorization rather than on the meaning and importance of content information. When Mary Ann, an English instructor who uses an interdisciplinary approach to teaching, intended to teach a unit on Islam, she was informed by the administration that she was not to teach religions that were not aligned with Western Christianity. Therefore, although there are occasional sparks of pedagogical light at RMS, they are quickly shaped by curricular standards as informed by community expectations. With art relegated to the enrichment portion of the school day, the groundwork for its consideration as a "serious" semiotic system is already laid. The question remains as to how this footnoting of art is experienced in the pedagogical culture of RMS and what students bring to that experience.

Perceptions of Art at Riverview Middle School (or How to Minimize a Semiotic System)

The low status of art in the curricular system is not a novel situation. Report after report on the state of art education inevitably laments art's place in education and in society at large (American Association of University Women, 1992). Therefore, the relegation of art to the enrichment sector of Riverview's curriculum is, if anything, an institutional enactment of the *status quo*. But what of the particularity of art's place at Riverview? What can be inferred from the conditions in which art, as a semiotic system, is minimized and even dismissed? The confluence of circumstances at Riverview seems to offer up a sad set of lessons on how to minimize art.

Administrative and Faculty Antipathy

As Nespor's (1997) study indicates, the administrative direction set out by the school principal and the ways in which faculty take up curricular matters can have wide consequences. Riverview Middle School is not an exception to this pattern. At RMS, the secondary status of art in the school is demonstrated in subtle and sometimes overt ways. For instance, extracurricular contributions of faculty often are recognized in the form of a small stipend. For the art/talent show, the music teacher receives a stipend, but the art teacher does not, even though the art teacher is an organizer of the show. This might seem an oversight if not viewed in the context of the general lack of interest and even antipathy toward art at RMS. These dispositions are perhaps best recounted in the words of Louise Woolf, the art teacher, when she recalls a conversation she had with the principal:

Everything that the principal ever says to me concerning a compre-
hensive supportive approach to a fine arts program here at RMS is,
"We can't do. We can't do. We can't do." That's the basis of my frustration. I also said we've got to at least remodel the art room because
the numbers are up, even with me teaching the extra class. I said,
"Something has to break. We've got to do something."

He then said, "Well, you agreed to teach this extra class." I agreed
to it the year before, thinking it was a temporary thing. What happens
this year is that it not only gets repeated; it gets assumed that I will
just teach it across the board, both semesters. I was never asked.

Faculty members openly dismissed Louise's concerns about overcrowd-
ing in her art classes and, at a faculty meeting, one of the counselors suggested that she "change her curriculum" to accommodate the large numbers. This made Louise "so angry, so furious" that she asked the counse-
lor, "Hey, why teach art at all? I mean, why do we even bother?" To this,
other teachers "were laughing and then another staff member made a joke
about just teaching everybody orange, or green, or something."

Art as a Vehicle for Deviance

The minimization of art as a representational form may be tangled in another issue for adults at Riverview—that of the tension between culturally
valued visual representations and Christian fundamentalist values. At RMS,
some faculty members equate art with pornography and deviance. One
incident, in which the health teacher accused Louise Woolf of "traffick[ing]
in sexual pornography" by encouraging a young male to engage in porno-
graphic inquiry, illustrates this type of thinking particularly well. The incident is recounted by Louise Woolf:

The boy who checked out the book from the library was doing a research project. The book that he chose was age-appropriate and had
some nudes in it. The librarian bought it for the library because it is a
good series. The boy brought the book to class and showed it to me
right at the end of the class. He held it up and I saw the cover and said,
'Yes, that's the new Young Reader's series. It's supposed to be pretty
good. I haven't had a chance to look at it.' That's all I said to him. I
also told him that it was good that he found something on modern art,
which was the topic he was interested in. He told me the librarian
helped him find it.

So he left my class, went to health class, the next class, and he
apparently showed the book to the health teacher and told her that

there was a particular painting in it that made him feel uncomfortable. It was a painting of a nude. At any rate, the health teacher went to the vice principal and told him that I had brought in one of my personal books, had given it to the boy, and that I was having him do nude art for me. The obvious insinuation is that I had been leading him on. The vice principal, unlike others who might have immediately called social services, came down and asked me if I had given the kid any of my own books. There were a few minutes of confusion, and then it had dawned on me what had happened. The health teacher had gone to the vice principal to tell him that I had been promoting nudity. I talked with the vice principal and he took care of it.

Louise Woolf went on to offer her personal interpretation of this sequence of events:

I think this incident said more about what she [the health teacher] really thought about me, what kind of person I was. I think her beliefs were operating to help her construct this text or this narrative about what had gone on because the library sticker was on the outside of the book. I mean, it was more than obvious that this was not my book, if she had bothered to really look at the book. . . or if she even bothered to talk with the boy at length about it.

Whether the idea of art as pornography is located for the teachers in the school, in the artwork, or in the person of the art teacher (as opposed to the librarian) and what she represents is an open question. But clearly the message concerning the danger of this representational medium was apparent. With sixth graders on the cusp of adolescence and just beginning to be permitted to be considered as sexual beings, the artworks in the library book may have offered up more than the aesthetic—hence the triple moment of the culturally valued aesthetic image, the student's discomfort, and repression of the sexual by adults who read the image through the lens of fundamentalist Christian beliefs.[4]

Art as Functionless

Whereas some at RMS may see art as the "tool of the devil," others, in particular some students, see art as relatively meaningless. Of course, sign systems are but irrelevant spots on paper or awkward forms if they hold little or no meaning for the interpreter. Moreover, telling someone that something is useful never is quite as effective as when the person discovers and/or witnesses the functionality themselves. Some of Louise Woolf's former students (eighth graders at the time of the study) speak directly to this issue in an interview with Peggy Albers:

> *Peggy*:   Brad, tell me what you think of art.
>
> *Brad*:   I don't like art because I don't think it serves a purpose. It's not like I'm going to grow up and be an artist. It's not worth it to me. Especially abstract art. *[He shows Peggy his abstract sculp-ture—it is a bloodshot eyeball painted white with a large indented hole—almost as if the pupil of the eye had been shot through]*. This is prob-ably my best piece.
>
> *Peggy*:   Why don't you think that art serves a purpose?
>
> *Brad*:   I don't have an interest in art. Ms. Woolf says that there is art all over like in shoes and T-shirts and stuff. I take lots of things for granted. Like shoes. Ms. Woolf says that's like art, but I consider art a way to express yourself.
>
> *Peggy*:   Shoes and T-shirts are not a way to express your-self?
>
> *Brad*:   Yeah, but shoes and T-shirts are not art. Not to me. To Ms. Woolf it is but she knows more. She probably understands it better.
>
> *Peggy*:   What do you think that art is then?
>
> *Brad*:   Art is stuff that people like to look at. Like paint-ings and stuff.
>
> *Peggy*:   Why don't you like art?
>
> *Brad*:   It's never been a large part of my life.

Eddie:	There's no use for art. People like slap down stuff and they get lots of money for it. *[He refers to the Kandinsky poster on the wall of the art room.]*
Peggy:	What do you mean by that, Eddie?
Eddie:	Picasso did a whole head and it's pretty stupid. It's a half head inside a head—kind of like two images. Why should they get money for that?
Brad:	Tell her what you said yesterday about your baby cousin.
Eddie:	My baby cousin can do better than this.
Jason S:	If people get money for abstract art, other people should get it like us. We can draw stuff as good as them.
Eddie:	I don't like abstract art.
Jason H:	Art isn't just paintings. It's music and stuff.
Jason S:	I like the kind of art like music and TV.
Peggy:	Why is that?
Jason S:	More people listen to it. They can watch it. It is right there.
Peggy:	But why is music more accepted as good art than paintings and such?
Randy:	More people listen to it and can understand music. When you see art, you can't understand it. It doesn't relate to what we're doing.

Brad: It doesn't relate to us.

Randy: It's just painting. It just hangs there.

Jason S: Art is looking at pictures. Drawings and paint-
               ings.

This discussion excerpt illustrates how the general conceptualization of
art as "high culture," the art of museums and art galleries, can be dismissed. It illustrates that Ms. Woolf, despite her good efforts, has not con-
vinced these adolescents that we live in a world of visual culture, a world
in which art as a visual semiotic is everywhere, a world wherein the aesthetic decorative function of artwork can be found in sites as diverse as T-
shirts and cereal boxes, a world in which the artwork in advertisements
becomes an index for the tolerance of social commentary about race and
sexuality. Ultimately, the students' perceptions about art's lack of functionality is a perception of a particular conceptualization of art, a
conceptualization that may limit their explicit understanding of its place,
perhaps limiting their view of the possibilities of art as a semiotic system.

Art As a Site of Pedagogical Abuse

Nearly all of the students who entered Louise Woolf's classroom in sixth
grade reported that they had not had positive experiences in elementary art
classes. They very openly shared their feelings about their art teachers,
how these teachers talked about and worked with them and their art, and
how their artworks were viewed. These stories generally speak to the art
teachers' disinterest in helping students become better artists. Two elementary art teachers, Ms. Henry and Mr. Mason, feature prominently. The
students' recountings of these experiences represent a conflagration of
negative affect and ideas about art that cannot be disentangled because
these experiences are seen through the lens of memory and the protective
work that memory does.
     Kim talks about Ms. Henry:

> I remember last year really well. I had a teacher who wasn't very nice.
> She wasn't the kind of teacher that would run around and tell every-
> one their work was bad but she hollered all the time. I just didn't like
> her. She had a really bad attitude. Kids that had trouble, she didn't

really help. She was just there. If we couldn't do our work, she'd send kids out in the hall.

Carolyn, also having worked with Ms. Henry, states: "She was mean. She didn't care. She was mean but that's okay. She didn't know what abstract was. She made Laura throw her abstract artwork away. In grade school, Ms. Henry used to throw our stuff away." Julie summarizes the experiences of many of these students: "We did paintings that the teacher told us to do. We had to do what she told us. If she told us to make a mask, we had to do it exactly like she said."

Yet, Ms. Henry's attachment to art of a certain type, a type indecipherable by many students, remains fixed in students' minds, and only serves to add to the mystification of art as a semiotic system. What is even more troubling is that excelling in the semiotic system of Ms. Henry's world meant relinquishing the literal ownership of the artwork, as the following discussion among students illustrates:

Patty: If the people did good, she would keep your work and she would put it in the showcase.

Nina: Yeah, and then you never got it back.

Patty: It seems like we never got anything back.

Charlotte: She would tell you you'd get it back and then the year would be over and you wouldn't get it back. It seems like you never get anything back. And the only people that she put in there were really good.

The other art teacher, Mr. Mason, also seemed to work from a position of an authoritarianism that disregarded students as learners. Added to this authoritarianism was the language of sexual stereotyping. Ironically, Stacey partially echoes back the sexual stereotype she witnessed as she critically recalls her early work with Mr. Mason:

We did a lot of sculpture because he was a man teacher and all's he wanted to do was build things. He'd say, "You girls probably can't do these things and the boys can."

When asked about her response to this type of comment, Stacey replied
that that she would say:

> "I can do this *[giggle]*." And some of the girls' [work] did turn out
> better than the boys'. If you couldn't do this then he'd make you just
> stand in the hall. Like if you needed help in doing something, you'd
> just have to do it. He'd say, "I'm not going to help. You just have to do
> it." When we would ask where the paper is, he'd just say. "You should
> know how to do this kind of stuff." We'd just have to sit there the
> whole period and then get in a lot of trouble.

Celia agrees with Stacey: "He was mean. If you didn't do things his
way, he got mad." Frieda's experience was similar: "He said that he didn't
like what I did and that I didn't follow directions and that if I didn't do my
art over then I would get an F." Emily, who was observed to be a careful
and thoughtful student in Louise Woolf's class, said, "He ripped a paper
up because my sky did not touch the ground all the way." Katrina's experience mirrors that of her female colleagues:

> I remember he said, "What's that?" When I told him that it was a dog
> that I was making for my mother for Mother's Day, he just said, "You
> can't do that in here now. I told you to make a vase. Didn't you see the
> one I made on the counter? That's what you have to do. If you want to
> do anything else, do it outside my class. Anyway, you didn't make the
> dog right. The proportion is all wrong. See the head is way too big and
> the back legs couldn't hold up his weight." Then he took it and squashed
> it.

Larry had a different experience with this teacher:

> He always had teacher's pets. If you were a teacher's pet, you got
> away with murder. I was one of them. I liked [Mr. Mason]. He let me
> do whatever I wanted as long as I did sculpture. I got good grades no
> matter what I turned in or how it looked. It was fun.

Whether Ms. Henry and Mr. Mason's reactions were a response to
their own discomforts or inadequacies with teaching art or whether they
were dispositionally mean spirited, their interactions with students in art
classes left indelible marks on students' perceptions of what art was and
their own competencies with it. Even the boys who won Mr. Mason's favor retained a working definition of creating representations in art that

was restricted largely to sculpture. Additionally, the seeming refusal of these teachers to elaborate, through demonstration and coaching, how students could become literate in art very likely contributed to the loss of power that students may have felt when they had to think of themselves as people who could use this semiotic system for their own purposes to represent their own meanings. Together, these issues indicate how students began to build a disposition about art (Arnstine, 1995). For the students entering Louise Woolf's class, enabling new dispositions in the face of the students' pedagogical and social histories would appear to be a daunting task.

Longing for Art

Yet, despite the antipathy, social perversity, and psychic abuse that seemed to be associated with art, it was also the case that many students longed for the kind of opportunities that art as a semiotic system could offer. Many students talked of liking to draw and of the opportunity to "let my mind go off." The possibilities of working within the semiotic system of art and representing their interpretations of their world and their senses of themselves in it were more powerful than the emotional aftereffects of the time when "The teacher tore up my paper."

Students were willing to continue to acknowledge that "I like sitting down and drawing (out of my mind or looking at something)." They recognized that there were other art experiences besides those they had experienced in elementary school. As one student reflected on her art experiences: "They've been good except for elementary education. They made me hurry up but I like to take my time." Memories of art being "boring" or of "bad/mean art teachers" lingered despite student comments that they they liked art and drawing, using their imagination, and making things they "can be proud of."

However, despite the strong positive affect students remembered toward the creation of art, many students also said that they "were not good at art." This latter perception may have come from being told by the teacher that their pictures "weren't very good" or from situations in which "if [you] made a mistake on your artwork, she would yell at you. It wasn't very fun." Yet, nearly all students indicated that they longed to learn more about art.

In journal entries students made at the beginning of their work with Ms. Woolf, nearly all students spoke of wanting to develop better art skills, and to become better at "drawing, painting, and sculpting." Girls tended to want to work with and know more about colors, paints, clay, and wire. The boys wanted to work with and know more about models, cartoons, clay, and drawing. Their wish for Ms. Woolf: "Just don't make art boring."

The longings students had about art indicated that they were not yet ambivalent toward art, and, in that sense, they were not yet lost (Britzman, 1998). The ground was set, then, for their art teacher, Louise Woolf, to enter into this complexity of locations, loss, and longings; but before exploring the learning engagements that occurred at RMS under Ms. Woolf's tutelage, we take a moment to locate Louise Woolf and her own relationship to art.

Locating Louise:
Her Path to Artistic Possibility

As the art teacher into whose classroom sixth-grade students entered with hopes for artistic possibilities mixed with recent pedagogical histories that minimized art, and with biographies that included a social fabric made up of the incendiary mixture of Christian fundamentalism, racism, and homophobia, Louise's past represents, in many aspects, a litany of counterpoints. Cherokee, mixed class, lesbian, and artist are all labels that Louise used in identifying herself. Her identifications with these marginalized identities all contributed to how she engaged students and what was possible for her as a teacher and, more particularly, as a teacher of art. As Greene (1978) suggested, the genealogy of our perspectives is important because "all of this underlies our present perspectives and affects the way we look at things and talk about things and structure our realities" (p. 2).

Identity Embodied

Louise Woolf was born in a moderately sized university town of approximately 40,000 people. Her father was a trained architect and owner of a limestone business, and her mother was a nurse. Her father, of Scottish descent, married Louise's mother, a Cherokee/African American, against the wishes of his own immediate family. Life was emotionally difficult for Louise: There was a continual clash of class difference, stemming from her father's wealthy background and her mother's impoverished one. At the age of 3 years, Louise's only escape from the constant fighting lay beneath her father's drafting table. It was here that she first explored art:

I knew that by the time that I was 3 years old I was keeping a portfolio. I can't remember doing that. My parents say that. But by the first time I was able to crawl to the first Crayola, I would draw and mark with pencils and crayons. My dad's an architect so there was always paper around. I always thought his Dietzen drawing table, the big drawing table which I now have, was pretty cool with the French curves, and his mechanical pencils. I disliked my family so much that I pretty much lived underneath that most of my life. I had a little drawing board under there that I put across the foot braces. So literally from age 3, I crawled under this huge table to get away from them. I come from a really loud dysfunctional family. There is never any sense of security in knowing that you could park yourself in the family room and not end up having some huge fight ensue over you. And I didn't like my older sister. So, I just sort of hid out under this big drawing table as much as I could to find peace of mind. I always drew and I always liked to draw. I think that because of my family's dysfunction and out of pure boredom, I practiced drawing and developed skills that were way beyond where they should have been developmentally.

The class differences about art between her father and mother grew deeper as Louise became older. Louise's father, whose family frequented art museums, often belittled Louise's mother and her Native American experience with art. Art, to Louise's mother, was utilitarian, not something that elevated a person to a higher social status. This chasm, in part, shaped Louise's own beliefs about art:

[With] my mom's family being Cherokee, art played a completely different purpose. Certainly, I think [this was] because she was one of the first generation born off the reservation into overwhelming poverty. My mom aspired to get a picture that matched the couch. That kind of thing. She didn't really have the background that my dad's family had. [They] came from the East coast, were patrons of the arts, and had access to museums. My mom's family didn't have that. So, class and social dynamics played out in the house. My dad would ridicule my mom for not appreciating my art or anybody else's. Then, at the same time, she just couldn't get it [because] she came from a background where art is more utilitarian. She understood it on one level, but on another level, she missed the boat completely. She was unable to conceive of art in a Western sense—something that gets elevated as something above and beyond that which gets hung on the wall and exalted, that doesn't serve some kind of utilitarian purpose even if it's spiritual. So, anyway there was always that dynamic. I would be aggravated by her but, at the same time, feel sorry for her because of my dad's rudeness. When we'd go to museums, my mom didn't engage with the art very much. [Then] my dad would always lecture her on what was wrong with her and how "stupid" she was. I think I became sensitive to class distinctions and appreciation, abilities, or inabilities to engage with the arts. I really think that was the beginning. I always tried to get my mom to understand or appreciate my art more and, even to this day, she doesn't quite understand why someone would want to be an artist in the Western sense. I think that is what got me looking at class distinctions even though I maybe couldn't have articulated it that way at that time.

Louise's family experiences with art, both as utilitarian and as a means to elevate status, offered her insight into her own "abilities and inabilities" to engage with art. Because her relationship with her father was "miserable," Louise would often work hard at art just to "get approval or any kind of feedback or elicit a response from him that was at all positive." She continued to draw and become better, so when she began school, her art skills were far beyond those of her classmates.

School as Meaningful Interference

Art class, like her general education, was not challenging for Louise. In elementary school, art was "mostly cut and paste, and draw and crayon and that sort of thing. I remember being disappointed and frustrated by the projects that we did." This cut and paste approach was largely done because her elementary teachers were not trained artists. Monday morning, though, was her favorite time. She was free to decorate her weekly folders as she chose. Her elementary teachers, Louise recalls, did not appreciate the subject matter and wanted to control Louise's expression. In fact, one of her teachers went so far as to contact Louise's parents about how disturbing the artwork on her folders was:

> My folders would be elaborate artistic achievements. Two of my folders got me into trouble. They were back to back. My first grade teacher called my parents for a conference because I had illustrated the Wizard of Oz and on one side was the castle and the witch. The monkeys were flying out against a dark sky and the perspective was just incredible. The monkeys had landed on the other side of the folder and were ripping the scarecrow apart. I'm sure this speaks to the family violence that I grew up in. It was therapy for me, I guess. I followed it the next week with a scene of dinosaurs fighting on a cliff. A tyrannosau-

rus rex had ripped the side off a brontosaurus and was flinging it over the mountain. [This], again, speaks to the violence and dysfunction at home. The teachers would marvel over my work and I always got to do the bulletin boards and that kind of thing. At the same time, they didn't really like my expression and wanted to control that. But that was the last straw and the teacher told my parents that she was worried about me psychologically. I think back about it [and wonder] if the bruises on my arms had anything to do with it. [The teacher] never mentioned those. She just thought the art was appalling. She told my dad that I should be drawing pictures of kittens and flowers the way the other girls were. My dad told her to leave me alone and she did after that.

Louise's junior high teachers "became particularly supportive" because she worked with them over several years even though she played several "outrageous" pranks. Yet, a frustration in Louise's early experiences lay, in part, in the distinctions teachers seemed to have for what boys and girls should do in her art classes:

I was clearly not making the kind of art that a little girl should make in the teacher's opinion. But somewhere along the line, she would have been socialized to expect certain things. I think a lot of what Sadker and Sadker, that's a husband and wife [research] team, write about teacher gender-based expectations of their students. Boys will get more of the teacher's attention, and I think that is true. They act out more, they take ownership for the space more, they ask more questions without raising hands. They are in your face more generally moving out of assigned space so they'll come up for more help than the girls. So, all the way around, I see the potential of boys theoretically to get more help in art education classes than girls.

Privileges based on gender in art construction and expression were evident to Louise very early in her schooling. From her construction of violent scenes with dinosaurs in first grade to her use of clay and sculpture in high school, Louise challenged stereotyped constructions of what male and female artists do and with what media.

Whereas her teachers seemed set to interfere with or question some of the meanings she represented in her artworks, a major discouragement for Louise lay in her art teachers' inability to offer her any sort of critique, to push her talents beyond where they were. When Louise asked her art teachers how she could make her artwork better, they merely responded, "Why

do you want to make this better? That's so good anyway." Her art teachers knew little about technique and helped her realize later that in public
schools "art education instruction and technical expertise were grossly
lacking." Louise's explanation for this is as follows:

> Most of the teachers were art educators. They really didn't practice
> art, and didn't have an art background. [They] didn't go beyond tak-
> ing above and beyond a few courses in drawing, painting, or ceram-
> ics. Just to learn how to fire a kiln and mix clay. Anyway, they didn't
> have the expertise to teach me. So, they would praise my work, but
> they couldn't critique it and help me move beyond that. Art educators
> don't have to have technical skills development to teach basic prin-
> ciples of art, which is, I think, ridiculous. They try to teach you but
> don't have the technical skills necessary to prepare you for college or
> for even being successful in the classroom. I believe that a good artist
> educator, and good teachers in general, give kids guidelines so they
> don't feel lost but, at the same time, give them a lot of creative free-
> dom so that they can explore their own interests and make things mean-
> ingful.

Louise decided in high school that she wanted to pursue an art degree
in college. She sought out programs that satisfied her desire for " a con-
centration of fundamentals education." She went on to say, "I think I received that. My work changed drastically . . . I definitely had some of my
technical questions answered. The emphasis was on art history, English,
writing, expressive modes of learning in language, and that was the format
that I wanted." From her experiences, Louise saw several key elements in
art education that were important to her: getting good technical training,
integrating other modes of expression, constructing critiques, and connecting art education to the real world of art.

Louise's backgound offers several interesting insights into her perspectives on learning and art. Louise has a strong appreciation for the contribution of educational research to teaching. She discusses class distinctions in art, and offers insight into art education informed by feminist and
critical research (American Association of University Women, 1992;
Fausto-Sterling, 1985; Gilbert & Taylor, 1991; Thorne, 1993; Walkerdine,
1990). Sadker and Sadker's (1984) work, directly mentioned by Louise,
focuses on gender inequality in schools, which Louise finds important in
her own practice. Louise values the importance of personal expression, or
voice, in the representation of meaning and its connection to stereotypes
surrounding gender. This issue, again, points to a myriad of research on

voice from both sociopsycholinguists such as Harste, Short, and Burke (1988) and those engaging in feminist work on gender and education (Britzman, 1991; Orner, 1992; Pagano, 1990). Without having a teacher with an artist educator's background, Louise argues that learners become bored or frustrated with art because both technique and the freedom to explore meanings in artistic representations are important. Finally, Louise believes that students need supportive critique to encourage talent, rather than harsh criticism. Her early schooling experiences shaped, in part, Louise's concept concerning the role of an artist educator and now inform her middle school art pedagogy and practice.

Louise did not become a teacher until her late thirties. Her own early experiences with art and her desire to reshape assumptions about art in schools were instrumental in her choice to become an educator:

> I fell into education because it was something that I had an interest in, more or less, thinking that it needed to be critiqued and revitalized, and art education needed to be connected to the real world of art. So there were several reasons, but largely because I wanted to have more fulfilling work and wanted to have time for my art. Education seemed to be a good way to go.

Louise, then, although markedly different from her students in innumerable ways, seems to share with them ideas about art, the importance of technique and form, and the freedom to create artistic representations that speak of their desires, thoughts, and imaginings.

Locational Clashes and Pedagogical Potholes

Louise as the only art teacher at Riverview Middle School teaches all sixth-, seventh- and eighth-grade students. As Louise assumed her identity as the art teacher at RMS, she automatically moved into the marginal space to which art teaching was relegated. However, Louise also made decisions about the other marginalized identities that she would name or cloak in silence.

One identity she named was that of her Cherokee ancestry. The reaction of teachers and students to this knowledge revealed not merely a gap, but a clash between world views:

> I always told [the students] that I felt more aligned with Cherokee customs and beliefs, even though I wasn't a practicing Cherokee according to the government statistics. [The students] would just feel like I was devoid of something or they would always ask me things

that were stereotypical. [This stereotypical] view of Indians was up-
held by Mr. Christianson [the history teacher] all the time [when] he
mocked Indians. [The students] would ask me things like, "Are you
civilized?" or wasn't I worried that I couldn't go to heaven?

With reactions such as these, it is no wonder that Louise hid her identity as
a lesbian to protect herself:

That's another piece of discomfort that I felt. I couldn't be open there
[at Riverview]. I knew there was no way I could, I guess. I went into
the job knowing what the community was like, but also was smart
enough to stay closeted. And then as time went on, in very quick order, I realized that there was no way I could come out to anyone there,
and I never did.

The potential pedagogical potholes that might be created through both
Louise's naming and silence are best foreshadowed in her own words in a
lesson she conducted with her own students:

Aesthetics has to do with the beautiful and useful. It deals with what you
find beautiful. Aesthetics is about your own personal beliefs, values, and
philosophy about life. *[Louise moves to a student wearing a sports T-
shirt and points to the shirt.]* That's an aesthetic decision. When you
choose clothing for color, emblems, words, you are making aesthetic decisions. Something made you choose one shirt over another. You made
artistic decisions about your opinions about what to buy. It's important to
find out what your beliefs are. Think about art in an expanded way.

In this brief talk, Louise connects aesthetics with her students' lives. She
pushes them to think about art not just as paintings that hang on walls, but
as continual experiences that surround them and about which they make
daily decisions. Her experiences form part of her aestheticism, an aestheticism that is markedly different from that of Riverview. How Louise
and her students took up the satisfaction of student longings with respect
to learning technique and form and the issue of aesthetics and interpretation is the substance of the next two chapters.

NOTES

[1] Several sources were used to obtain information about the community of Riverview and its surrounding area. Because of the need to maintain the confidentiality ensured to participants, none of
these documents is referenced in the reference list of this book.

[2] The source is not referenced in order to protect the confidentiality assured the participants.

[3] The breakdown of the denomination of churches includes the following: one Catholic, Episcopalian, Lutheran, Methodist, Presbyterian, Jehovah's Witness, several Baptist, and about 20 evangelical Christian churches.

[4] See Steiner (1995) for a discussion of art in an age of conservatism. Steiner addressed, in particular, issues such as what constitutes pornography in the context of a discussion of the Mapplethorpe exhibit and considers issues related to artworks and the interpretations that are made of them.

FREEDOM, FORM, AND FEEDBACK

Frank: I put the clouds up here.

Ms. Woolf: Uh huh. Good.

Frank: Do you think it's good?

Ms. Woolf: Good? It's a haunting feeling, the way you did the sky. I like that. Yeah, that's good.

Frank: Is that what's that called? The border line?

Kane: Horizon line.

Frank: Is that done right?

Ms. Woolf: Yeah, that looks fine. Then this would be your night sky, you know, coming down to this point, and then this is just the ground going back.

This vignette illustrates how freedom, form, and feedback intersect in students' representational work. Frank used what he knew about form to create a "border line," a tool artists use to express perspective. He freely expressed his choice of topic for his artistic representation through a landscape, and he received feedback from both Ms. Woolf and Kane.

In this chapter, we focus on freedom, form, and feedback as we explore art as literacy. In essence, we explore the enablement of meaningful and valued visual representation for the sixth graders at RMS. We consider how Ms. Woolf, the sixth-grade art teacher, created a pedagogical situation in which her focus on the freedom she allowed students as they worked artistically, the skills she emphasized as they created artistic forms, and the feedback she and fellow students provided to students satiated some of their artistic longings.

Like the opening vignette, much of the data we present illustrates the entanglement of freedom, form, and feedback. Although we present each aspect separately to highlight its particularity and to demonstrate its specific role in the artistic development of the sixth-graders at RMS, it is inevitable that all the elements permeate the discussion.

Studio Sensibilities: Liberating Constraints

As Dewey (1938) said, everything depends on the quality of the experience, and the experience that Ms. Woolf decided to create for her students was not that of a classroom in which art is the interloper, but that of a studio wherein the physical and social environment is structured to invite art. As sixth-grader Cassie said: "When I entered this classroom, I immediately knew that it was an art room." The physical space and the kind of engagement it allowed was a counterpoint to other physical spaces in the school.

In Ms. Woolf's classroom, 14 black surface tables were arranged semicircularly in pairs, with up to four students at each table. The table arrangement was deliberate to encourage and support partner work, peer work, or both. The paired tables offered enough space for students to work with large pieces.

Besides ample space for their work, students had available at any moment the many art media they might need to explore their visual representations of meaning. Unlike their other elementary school classrooms, Ms. Woolf's classroom had readily available a variety of tools that supported drawing, painting (acrylic, oil, and pastel), multimedia, and clay and paper sculpting. Ms. Woolf left all the media out for students to use because she assumed that she could not predict when an individual student might need particular media to complete a piece of art. Students were free to move about the room to collaborate with others, seek feedback on their artworks, and secure needed art materials.

In the same way that artists surround themselves with a bank of materials such as books, magazines, pictures, and slides to explore their literacy in art, Ms. Woolf provided similar, readily accessible materials for the students in her class. How-to-draw art books for areas such cartoons, animals, airplanes and birds; books and magazines on composition, drawing, painting, sketching, and sculpting; boxes of art prints labeled "people," "animals," and "landscapes"; and a slide projector with a library containing hundreds of slides of artists' works were all available reference items in the classroom. Posters on the walls reminded students of art vocabulary, the elements of design, and directions on how to do journal critiques.

In essence, the classroom space was filled with expectancies—that students would collaborate in either creating or commenting on artworks, that students would choose from an array of materials available depending on their artistic and representational needs, and that students would seek out resources to help them think through representations and their effects. The constraints of the classroom were much different from those of the past wherein materials were meted out like precious gems and talk was seen as a betrayal of the rules. In contrast to the students' classrooms of the past, Ms. Woolf's room, with its underlying studio structure, read as a space of intellectual freedom and artistic choice. But this portrayal should not be taken to mean that the classroom operated without constraints. The expectancy for students to take up the invitation to work as artists in a studio-like context was itself a constraint. However, Ms. Woolf's classroom atmosphere benefited from being a counterpoint in the school whereby she replaced one set of physical and social structures with another.

Ms. Woolf extended her system of liberating constraints in the way she worked with the art curriculum as well. She explicitly invited students to become coparticipants in the organization of their own artistic experiences. On the first day of class, Ms. Woolf asked her students to create and write in personal artist journals. For their initial entries, students were asked to respond to whether they liked art, describe their previous experiences with art, and project what they would like to learn in this art class. Ms. Woolf used student responses to gain insight into her students' experiences with art and to guide her decisions about curriculum. As she said to her students on the first day:

> I tailor the class to fit your needs. After I read your journals, I'll design the curriculum or write lessons that will use your interests. We

don't use a textbook that gives you examples. We'll use your own interests. As long as I teach these art elements and principles that the state requires, and I do this well, we can do whatever we want. You have a lot more power in your learning because we are partners. We'll talk about your work and work on art skills together. Over time, you'll get better with things. I call that problem solving. The emphasis in this class is to become a better thinker and problem solver. You're expected to think about the process, not just [crank] out art pieces. I'm trying to find ways to value your thinking.

Ms. Woolf's students became "curricular informants" (Harste, Woodward, & Burke, 1984) as their comments were taken by her to shape the curriculum.

The freedom to work in similar kinds of conditions as artists in an art studio was a challenge for some. Boys, much more often than girls, showed their resistance to art class by disrupting class procedures and vandalizing artworks and property. Ms. Woolf encouraged movement within the art room so as not to disturb the process of constructing visual meaning (e.g., getting materials, asking for help), yet, some boys interpreted this as time to move about the room and disturb others. As Ms. Woolf tried to deal with these intrusions, some boys tended to disregard Ms. Woolf's role as teacher, taking advantage of the freedom that she offered. In this representative scene, Ms. Woolf interrupted her talk with a student to address boys who were not focused on their work:

> *Bart*: I was thinking about the basketball. I'm going to go over these lines with a different color. I'm going to have people put their finger prints on and around it.
>
> *[Mark and Phil are moving around the room aimlessly, interrupting others' work by leaning over their shoulders, poking each other, and not attending to their own work.]*
>
> *Ms. Woolf*: You guys, if you are going to be in here, don't get anything going with those guys. I think that is neat, Bart. To me, when I look at that, I feel like there are all kinds of energy moving fast in front of me. . . . *[She moves to the two boys.]* Okay, you two guys. Listen to me. We need to

talk. Have I asked you three times—no, come here. Three. No, don't give me that. Have I not asked you three times to sit down?

Mark: Yeah.

Ms. Woolf: Where do you think you have to be now?

Phil: In my seat.

Collins' (1995) work suggests that because art often is identified as a "feminine" course that develops only the emotional side of a person, boys often find little value in doing art or "women's work." Consequently, one way to read the boys' aggression is to see it as an immature but overt attempt to preserve their masculinity in the face of the subject matter. Indeed, as suggested in chapter 6, in some instances, male proficiency in art is associated with being gay, so acting out would be a means of asserting heterosexuality.

In addition to disrupting lessons, some boys vandalized other students' artworks or created a mess in the art room. For example, Ms. Woolf had to speak to five boys who had thrown clay all over the ceiling. She shared her frustration with Peggy:

> These boys got the clay out of the bucket and threw [clay] on the ceiling. So, I made them pick it up. I don't even know how to perceive of it. I'm whipped when it comes to trying to understand why anyone would decide to do that. It makes you wonder. What have I done to them to make them do this. Is it a personal attack? Or do they hate me? Are they having a bad day? What's the deal?

Through this action, the boys acted out their masculinity through aggression and their sense of self-confidence. In some way, they may have known that this, like other incidents at the school, would be viewed as their being just "boys." Their belief that art is a useless subject area (see chapter 3) may have prompted them to react in violent and aggressive ways. Unfortunately, these aggressive actions sometimes turned into acts of vandalism toward others' artworks. Although Ms. Woolf went to the office to share information with the administrators about the boys' vandalism, the boys were never disciplined by the school administrators for their actions.

Despite these resistances, Ms. Woolf's liberation of the constraints that had characterized students' prior experiences of art created the conditions for moving toward artistic possibility, toward experimentation with form, and even toward collaboration. Although these conditions also invited acting out behavior from some students, the vast majority welcomed the opportunities that a studio atmosphere offered.

Finding Form: Liberating Representation

As Ms. Woolf's own experience as an art student had taught her, and as her students also echoed in their journals (see chapter 4), the experience of the studio is not enough, especially in a world that has not come to grips with widespread encouragement of each individual's artistry. As a consequence, Ms. Woolf consciously built her curriculum on two aspects: lesson goals that allowed students to experience art as a process, and demonstrations of artistic techniques. As RMS student journal excerpts foreshadowed (see chapter 4), Ms. Woolf's direction appeared to go some ways toward satisfying students who long to have art demystified for them, and who are on the cusp of losing interest because they can not find their way through technique to representation.

Lesson Goals

Ms. Woolf created a curriculum based on students' interests, constructing a series of lesson goals that helped students to layer their skills with each assignment. From students' interests, Ms. Woolf created a series of 8 to 12 lesson goals per term.[1] Lesson goals are problem-solving assignments in art that "center on art techniques and methods, knowledge of materials, and their usage" (Ms. Woolf, class minilecture). Lesson goals were sequential in that they helped each student function as "a thinking artist" (Ms. Woolf, class minilecture).

For Ms. Woolf, lesson goals operated on several levels. To begin with, the goals were process-oriented. That is, students were required to focus on the techniques and methods they used to complete the lesson goal. The aim of the lesson was not only to invite multiple interpretations using the techniques or methods of interest, but to enable each student to participate at his or her own skill level. Figure 5.1 illustrates one lesson goal in which students are invited to become landscape painters. A noticeable feature of the lesson goal in Fig. 5.1 is its attention to perspective, a key element in drawing realistically and a desired goal that many students discussed in their journals.

You are a landscape painter painting the most beautiful outdoor scene you have ever seen. Your goal is to develop a sense of depth/space/perspective in your painting that includes a foreground, middle ground and background.

_____ Background

_____ Middle ground

_____ Foreground

Note: Objects are larger in the foreground. They appear smaller as you look further away.

FIG. 5.1   Example of a lesson goal plan.

A second function of lesson goals was to allow students to interpret the goal according to their own experiences and interests. For the lesson goal in Fig. 5.1, for example, many of the boys chose to create landscapes that focused on sports or cars, whereas girls often chose subject matter dealing with animals and human relationships. In nearly all lesson goals, students chose their own subject matter and media, interpreting the assignment in ways that centered on their interests.

A third function of lesson goals was to provide students with opportunities to problem solve in art. Problem solving in art requires thoughtful attention to detail and time to explore alternatives. An example of how alternatives can be explored is found in this short excerpted dialogue from Alice and Mary, who were trying to work out a way to hold the wire petals of a large sunflower together:

Alice: How do you think we can hold these petals together?

Mary: We can try and wrap more paper around the wire.

Alice: Won't it get too thick?

Mary: I don't know. We can try.

The lesson goals in Ms. Woolf's classroom were unlike the lesson plan exemplars provided in many art books used to guide middle-grade art instruction. In these art books, students often are asked to follow step-by-step minute instructions resulting in a focus not on the process of making art, but on the object itself. The following example from Mittler and Ragans' (1992) *Exploring Art* is illustrative:

> Select a leaf that you would like to draw. On a large piece of white paper, draw the leaf with a pencil. Next, draw the same leaf in different places on the paper, using a different drawing medium each time. Turn the paper so that you fill the paper with leaves. Draw some large ones and then draw some smaller ones to fill the smaller spaces. As you work, notice that some media make broad lines, while others make fine lines. Use your imagination to come up with new ways to make a line with each medium *[Reference is made to specific figures in the text]*. . . . Experiment using broad-line media to make larger leaves and fine-line media to make smaller leaves.
>
> Place the finished drawings up for study by the class. Can you tell what media other students used in their works? Does everyone's look the same? Why or why not? (p. 33)

Ms. Woolf saw such a product-oriented approach as problematic, expressing her belief as follows:

> A lot of the textbooks in art education were initially written for teachers who did not know how to teach art. They may be covertly written for the classroom teacher who is not an artist, and for the life of me, I don't know how in the hell you teach art if you are not an artist and do not know technique.

Ms. Woolf believed that "unlearning" (Wink, 1997) bad experiences in any subject area can occur when students' interests are centered.

The students at RMS liked the lesson goals approach. In contrast to their grade school experiences, students saw lesson goals not only as offering them ways to improve art literacy, but as providing them with choice in subject matter and media.

> *Brooke*:   The lesson goals don't make us do anything specific. They give us choice.
>
> *David*:   Options. In grade school art, they made us do things.

> *Brooke*:   We can choose from all sorts of things—paints and stuff.

> *Allison*:   I agree with all of that. We do things that our friends do but we can change it. We'll do the same thing at the table, but we'll say what we can do better. I've learned a lot this year. I can do stuff a lot better.

Lesson goals were the curriculum's core, designed from student input to help students build a knowledge base about the techniques and methods artists use to become better at their art.

Demonstrations

Ms. Woolf's studio art class was organized in such a way that students had maximum time to work on assignments and maximum opportunity to collaborate with others. Part of this collaboration involved Ms. Woolf, as a practicing artist, presenting demonstrations that had the potential to offer students insight into how artists begin and work through their art piece. Demonstrations show what one artist might do, for example, to create the illusion of depth through shading. Unlike step-by-step instructions found in an art book, demonstrations open up ways in which learners can think and work through a similar technique. Step-by-step instructions force a learner to eliminate choices, and subsequently relinquish control over how an artwork might look.

The studio art approach, in which demonstrations are central, focuses on the process of what the artist does to achieve a particular effect. A step-by-step instructional approach focuses on how the art piece will appear if a learner follows the directions. This emphasis on process works to open up students' minds to alternative ways of producing an artwork and alternative ways of interpreting various lesson goals. As Ms. Woolf says:

> When you are actually trying to function as a thinking artist, and when you focus on how artists learn and think in developing skills, that's where focusing on the learner as a problem solver begins. As I said, the artist has to go in and out of a picture, has to look at the whole, has to break the whole down and go into little parts of the whole, focus on those for awhile, come back out away from it, look at the whole again,

and how the parts function holistically again. So it's a movement in and out of a picture, in and out of imagery.

On days when students begin to work through a lesson goal, Ms. Woolf presented a demonstration of a technique. These usually lasted between 10 and 20 minutes. On subsequent days, Ms. Woolf presented what Lucy Calkins (1986) terms "mini-lessons," short and informative talks on particular art skills, techniques or methods that need further clarification and demonstration.

For example, if students were studying line technique and the lesson goal was to draw blind contours, Ms. Woolf demonstrated this art technique and the students then proceeded to work on this assignment. Next, the students worked on an assignment that incorporated newly learned skills with earlier learned skills. Finally, the students cleaned up their areas and discussed what they learned or what had caused them problems in terms of the lesson assignment.

For the most part, this was the schedule for Ms. Woolf's classes. However, on rare occasions, Ms. Woolf used nearly the entire 42 minutes of class time to demonstrate and talk about a technique that was particularly difficult. These instances included helping students learn to draw basic shapes, create an illusion of depth, and sketch figures. The following is an excerpt from one of these lengthier demonstrations. This demonstration was on figure drawing, a skill that many students wanted to improve:

[Ms. Woolf stands in the front of the class with chalk in hand. She is ready to talk to the students about this lesson, and to demonstrate figure drawing techniques.]

I think probably about 90% of you asked to do something with figure drawings, so we are going to do that. We are going to take 2 or 3 days to do some figure drawing. The reason I say 2 or 3 days is that you are going to be posing for each other. Now the way this works, lots of times teachers don't teach this age level anything about figure drawing because it is believed that it is too tough for you guys to figure out. I don't think that. I think, from what I've seen in your art work so far, that you are fully capable of doing this, but we are going to take it slowly, and we're going to break it down and make some sense out of it so that you will do a good job. This is because there is so much involved with figure drawing that we have to try to think through. . . .
[Ms. Woolf points to the guide.] It's just like the shaded drawing you did with still life blocks. You start out with the basic shapes. *[On the chalkboard, Ms. Woolf begins to draw ovals for the main*

torso of the body.] That's probably the most important thing to drawing anything, and you do the same thing with the human figure. You are probably wondering how you get beyond these basic shapes and start making it look like the real thing instead of a mannequin or a dummy. Well, we'll get to that. That's two or three steps from here. I'm up here at step one, showing the steps for setting up what's called a figure drawing. You'll hear these referred to as figure drawings, or human proportions drawings. . . .

In order to do a good job at this stage of drawing your person, you've got to make sure you use one of those real light sketchy lines. Remember assignment three in which you had to do those gesture studies? You moved your hand like this really fast on the paper *[She demonstrates the light and sketchy lines on the board.]* . . . . You want your line to be loose and sketchy so you can erase it. What I mean by that is you always start out drawing any human figure with just these basic shapes, but you draw the basic shapes so lightly and with such a loose sketchy line that when you go back and get ready to put clothes on the human figure you are able to erase the basic shapes. That's how you develop your figure drawing. I'm going to do an example here for you on the board (Fig. 5.2).

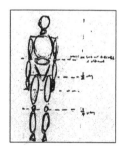 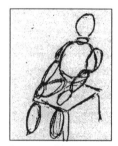

FIG. 5.2   Examples of Ms. Woolf's demonstrations of figure drawing.

In this particular lesson, several important aspects of the students' learning of art techniques and methods are evident. Ms. Woolf began with figure drawing, which is a form students want to learn. She encouraged her students to try hard, and reminded them that they are capable of drawing three-dimensional figures even though developmental research might argue otherwise. She connected some of the techniques (gesture and still life drawing) that students had learned earlier. Finally, Ms. Woolf offered students demonstrations on improving their figure drawing skills.

This format worked well for students. They not only were able to see improvement in their own work, but they could also teach and support each other as their skills evolved. Here is a representative example from a

still life exercise showing the kinds of talk that students engaged in as they
learned new techniques and skills:

> *[Three girls are working diligently at a table together. Their
> heads are bent over their papers, and their pencils moving
> slowly and deliberately. They appear to be taking to heart
> Ms. Woolf's verbal instruction, "Push for excellence." Ini-
> tially, they work individually on their still lifes, not saying a
> word to one another. One of the girls looks at her partner's
> piece. She makes a comment that, in turn, precipitates a
> longer conversation.]*

Martha: That's good.

Denise: It's not big enough. It's crooked.

Tess: Crooked?

*[They continue this conversation whispering to one another
so as not to disturb the quiet of the room.]*

Denise: *[To Tess]* Isn't that too big? *[She holds up her
              pencil to the still life and places her finger on it to
              measure the height of the cone.]* See, it's too big.

Tess: *[Tess measures the cone with her pencil and fin-
              ger as well. She closes one eye to get a better
              perspective on the height.]* I see now.

Peggy: *[To Martha]* That's looking good. Is the line tech-
              nique working?

Martha: It does for everything except the circle. I like
              this part. *[She points to the cylinder on which
              she is working. She points to the shading that
              she has done.]*

Denise: I like that. *[She points to Martha's cylinder.]*

Martha:	I don't. I can't use this. *[She puts down an eraser the size of a small chalkboard eraser.]*
Denise:	Here, use this.
Martha:	I used to have an eraser like this but it smells.
Tess:	It works.
Martha:	I like this, but the ball is too big. It looks like a basketball not a baseball.
Denise:	How do I do this? *[She refers to her circle and the technique of creating the roundness of it.]*
Tess:	Make the curve a bit more straight. Here, let me show you.

From a short demonstration on shading and shapes, Tess used what she learned about line technique to teach Denise how to create a more realistic looking baseball. In time, students learned from these demonstrations, presented demonstrations of their own to their partners, and subsequently became more literate in many art techniques and skills.

Although group demonstrations were efficient in presenting particular art skills or techniques to a large number of students at one time, many students needed additional individual demonstrations from Ms. Woolf to achieve their desired effect in working through the lesson goal. It was during these short individual art lessons that Ms. Woolf noticed what students could do in terms of skills, and then offered them further demonstration to help them build on the skills they were using to create their art piece.

For example, Ms. Woolf presented a large group demonstration on creating three-dimensional (3-D) pieces from wire. With this information in hand, Carl and Adam, partners collaborating on a wire sculpture of a car, needed more assistance in building their wire car. They found themselves at a roadblock and called Ms. Woolf over to help them think through how to stabilize the car:

Carl:	Ms. Woolf, could you help us? We want to attach this wire to this car.

Ms. Woolf: Now, how are you wanting to attach it?

Adam: Like this.

Ms. Woolf: Why don't we bring that one over here so you can look at it. *[Adam carries over a sculpture similar to the one on which they are working.]*

Carl: He's making the bottom.

Ms. Woolf: Be very careful, Adam. Here we go.

Carl: *[To Adam]* How big do we want to make this?

Ms. Woolf: Here's the example. *[She points to the example of the wire car.]*

Adam: I want to make it big. I want to make it big.

Ms. Woolf: This got bent a little bit. It's probably alright.

Carl: Can we have this go down here . . . like this?

Ms. Woolf: You could. We could rig it up with that. We'd probably have to put a dowel rod in it to get it to work and do it like a tinker toy. That would work better than the wire.

Adam: It would need some string, too.

Ms. Woolf: Yeah. I've got some string that would work. So start out with two circles that are the same size. One would be this circle. The other would be this circle and then. . .

Carl: Keep overlapping?

Ms. Woolf: Yeah. See how they've done it here? They come

back and forth wrapping around and then going
down again. Wrapping going up again.

Adam: Then they went around like that.

Ms. Woolf: Right. And then they went around like that. Can
             you see it there?

Carl: Yeah.

Ms. Woolf: See, you guys are actually acting like little engi-
             neers right now, building this. You are thinking
             like an engineer.

In this example, Ms. Woolf drew Adam and Carl's attention to several
techniques about working with wire. She brought over another artwork to
show them that artists often study similar artworks (the wire car made by
students in another class) to gain information about how to stabilize their
own wire sculpture. She drew on what the students had done well, and
then offered further demonstration of a technique such as wrapping wire
for stability. In the process, students began to notice this technique in artwork, such as Carl when he noticed the overlapping technique. Ms. Woolf,
in essence, showed Adam and Carl some of the tools that artists use in
working with this medium. Finally, before she left, she encouraged the
students by telling them what they were doing right. This verbal encouragement and individual instruction enabled students to become more pro-
ficient in using the tools of art.

In addition to further demonstrations on technique, students often
wanted ideas and suggestions to make their artworks more interesting.
Here Ms. Woolf, in helping Terry to work with her drawing, offered both
aesthetic and technical advice:

Ms. Woolf: Oh, this is good!

Terry: So after I get the figure drawn, I want to do the
             eyes.

Ms. Woolf: That sounds good. You know what would be
             neat? If you developed a background too, like

trees and stuff. It'll take us a few minutes to pick him out; he'll be camouflaged, and blend into the trees. That would be fun!

Terry: That's a neat idea. What else do you think I could draw? I was thinking about drawing my dad. I want to put him *[Referring to the figure she was working on]* next to my dad in this picture.

Ms. Woolf: Oh, that's a good idea. So you're going to draw your dad in there too?

Terry: Yeah.

Ms. Woolf: Great, that's great, the proportions look good on that figure.

Terry: Like that?

Ms. Woolf: Yeah you know like, like the size of the head and the length of the arms and legs. That looks really good.

Terry: One leg's kind of longer than the other leg.

Ms. Woolf: Actually it makes him look like he's stepping over something, or he's walking. It's fine.

This short exchange with Terry has several important implications. Initially, Ms. Woolf worked with Terry to help her think both aesthetically and technically about her work. But, as we can see from Terry's questions, she desired more than individual technical demonstrations. She wanted Ms. Woolf to help her think aesthetically about her piece. Optimal learning occurs in situations such as this in which Ms. Woolf provided feedback in the context of these representations.

In addition to learning from demonstrations by Ms. Woolf, students learned techniques from each other. Operating in a manner similar to that of Ms. Woolf, students demonstrated to each other various art techniques and skills. They examined their partners' artworks and suggested ideas that might improve them. In the following dialogue, Tracey demonstrated line technique to one of her partners, Carey:

> *[Three girls, Carey, Tracey and Lacey, sit together at a table. They have just begun to work with their realistic drawings of the still life blocks. The room is darkened, with the shades pulled down over the window.]*

Tracey:	That cube is really dark. It looks hard to draw but it's not. *[She erases some of what she has just drawn.]* This is my third eraser because everyone keeps stealing them. Man, my pencil broke!
Lacey:	They're hard to draw. *[Referring to the blocks]*
Carey:	How do your lines go like that?
Tracey:	You mean on the cylinder?
Carey:	Yes.
Tracey:	I'm not done with that. I keep messing up. *[Sitting back in her seat and looking at her still life.]* That looks like a house. *[Referring to the cube]*
Carey:	Can you show me how to draw that?
Tracey:	I'll draw it light in the corner. Don't go straight. Curve that, and do that with that. Hook those together. I think that's how I did it. I think that's how it looks. Because when you look at the side of a house, it doesn't always go straight. It curves up.
Carey:	Mine looks like a house. You didn't draw the line in the middle like that.

Tracey:	Here are some ebony pencils that'll give you the blacker black. *[Looking at Carey's artwork]* There's some overlapping here with the base-ball.
Carey:	Yeah, there is. *[Tracey gets up and moves to the still life table to have a closer look at the composition. She then returns to her table.]*
Tracey:	I probably won't be able to draw the stitches. That's good enough. *[She puts the finishing touches on one of her still life blocks.]*

As students internalized art skills and techniques for themselves, they gained confidence in their skills through partner demonstrations. This open sharing of demonstration and talk helped students enhance their literacy in art.

From the Exercise of Technical Skill
to Expressive Intentionality

As students in Ms. Woolf's class began to attend to each other's evolving texts, their talk moved into critical talk about their artworks. They began to consider more thoughtfully the relationship between technique and expression. Gradually, students began to assume more deliberate control over the kind of media they used to construct their artworks. Furthermore, they began to use various media to engage playfully with their friends and to solidify or change their social identity (how their work and they, as artists, are discussed). Thus, their artworks, in part, became their worlds. They began to feel free to release the expression within because they were more technically able to express this meaning.

Two sixth-grade students, Jesse and Abe, exemplified this sense of freedom of expression. Initially, they, like many of their classmates, were resistant to art. They did not believe they were good artists, and did not have any intention of working toward becoming better. However, over the course of their enrollment in Ms. Woolf's art class, they changed their perspective on art, themselves as artists, and their artworks.

Jesse and Abe, both randomly assigned to this class by the computer, had similar interests in music and masks. Like the rest of their classmates,

Jesse and Abe listened to Ms. Woolf's explanations and watched her demonstrations. However, in the fourth week of their class, they decided to collaborate on an artwork. Because they both liked the group KISS, they began to draft ideas on what they might construct as a wire sculpture. Drawing on what they knew about line technique, basic shapes, and gesture drawing, they decided to collaboratively create a wire sculpture of a guitar (see Figs. 3.8 and 3.9, chapter 3). They talked through how they wanted to make the guitar, and combined their two 10-foot wire pieces to construct it. Here, Jesse and Abe work through how they are going to stabilize their wire sculpture:

Abe: We're working on a guitar.

Jesse: It's a Gibson.

Abe: A Gibson guitar. *[They talk together about the positioning of a piece of wire for part of their guitar.]*

Abe: How about here?

Jesse: How about if we put it here?

Peggy: How did you get the shape of the guitar?

Jesse: We both worked on it. *[He points to the draft of their artwork, then continues to manipulate the wire into the shape of the bridge of the guitar.]* Well, we just both shaped it.

Abe: It was his idea of the real one. Then we just sort of put it together.

Peggy: How are you going to get it so that it stays in the shape of a guitar?

Abe: We're like gonna make a thing, a bridge or something like that, or Jesse said something about inside and outside. Ask him; he knows.

As Kress (1997) argued, representations start from a learner's point of interest in something. In this case, Jesse and Abe both had an interest in music and guitars. Both brought to the task different but complementary experiences with music. Jesse, like his father, played guitar and was in the process of starting a band. Abe also played guitar and read a great deal about musical groups and guitars. They began with an intentionality that directed their initial discussions, and moved them into figuring out how to create this artwork. They worked with the lesson goal to create a wire 3-D sculpture, had the freedom to interpret it given their own experiences and interests, and then proceeded to work on their artwork.

As Abe and Jesse talked about their 3-D construction, they drafted their ideas on paper. They began to work with the whole of the representation. Even though they had not yet begun to combine their wire to create this piece, they brought detail to their work through their draft. They talked about what they needed to do before they actually began the process of constructing this piece:

> *Jesse*: We have to have something here on the inside to keep it from going together, and something on the outside to keep it from going apart. *[He points to the bridge of the guitar and shows how they are going to keep the bridge from collapsing into a thin and distorted part of the guitar.]*

> *Abe*: These wires have to come down.

> *Jesse*: So it will hold its shape.

> *Peggy*: Oh, so it doesn't stretch or anything like that. This almost looks like its real size.

> *Abe*: Yeah, you can make it as big as you want to be. It was about that long, but we had to make it a little smaller. *[He holds out his arms to indicate the size of the guitar.]*

> *Jesse*: It was too hard, it was too hard to hold it together.

Abe: It was about that long and about that wide.

Peggy: Are you guys going to leave it as it is?

Abe: No, we are going to paint it red. . . . We're like
                 going to paint this right here, I think, white.

As these two young artists began to work out some of the details of their
construction, they opened themselves up to opportunities to hypothesize and
experiment with other art media (see Figs. 3.5, 3.6, and 3.7 chapter 3).

Jesse: Try to make your side the same as mine.

Abe: It won't look good if it is too pointed.

Jesse: Yeah. Right here. Take that down. That's not
                 working on that part. I think we will, like, paint
                 around the rest.

Abe: 'Cause there is no way we are gonna get the teeth
                 in there you know, like that. See 'cause there is
                 no way we are gonna make it. It like curves up.
                 We could make the teeth; maybe we can just color
                 them in. *[Both stop putting on papier mâché and
                 stand back to examine what they have done so
                 far in their sculpture.]*

Jesse: We probably could cut out the teeth. *[He points
                 to the draft of their piece.]*

Abe: Then the stuffing will come out from the back.

Jesse: Well, we're not really going to make a mask.
                 Well, sort of but . . .

Abe: Yeah, if we did cut it out. So what we could do
                 now is like draw with like a pencil and then we
                 could cut it out. *[Referring to the draft]*

Jesse:	Yeah, but we are gonna papier mâché over it.
Abe:	We could papier mâché and then draw like a mouth over it and then, and then . . .
Jesse:	Yeah, but see, even if we did, though, we need like the shape for the mouth like the lips where it comes out and stuff.
Abe:	Yeah . . .
Jesse:	Okay.

Jesse and Abe continued to work through their artwork by constantly hypothesizing about how their mask would look if they tried a particular technique. For example, as they tried to figure out how to put teeth on their mask, Abe suggested that they paint in the teeth, but Jesse proposed that they cut out the teeth. Abe picked up on Jesse's idea and elaborated by recommending that they draw the teeth first before cutting them out. They were able to test out this idea through drawing before they actually cut into their mask.

Along with hypothesizing and testing, students continually took risks as they consciously and unconsciously recognized an improvement in their own art skills. When students came to realize that they could communicate visually, it appeared that they relied less on the teacher for ideas and became confident in the choices they made as they constructed visual pieces. As the following short excerpt shows, Abe and Jesse made a number of artistic and technical decisions on their 3-D papier mâché mask before Ms. Woolf entered into their dialogue:

Ms. Woolf:	Do you guys need help? Oh my gosh, this is incredible! *[Ms. Woolf looks at the nose and touches it. The nose is flimsy. Abe and Jesse have taped the nose to the base of the head.]* Make sure you use tabs even on the nose.
Abe:	Okay. *[All the while Ms. Woolf talks to them, Abe and Jesse continue to layer the head with papier mâché.]*

Ms. Woolf: Yeah. And you don't need them to be very big on the nose. Like this. *[Ms. Woolf takes some paper, rips it, dips it in the glue mixture, and shows them how to place tabs on the nose area.]* Right and then otherwise the water in the papier mâché makes the tape just fall off and the nose would fall off.

Abe: Okay, okay.

Ms. Woolf: Yeah, and you might put a tab down this way, too. It would make it, that would make a better surface for papier mâché. This looks really nice you guys.

Jesse: Thank you.

Ms. Woolf: Yeah, that is turning out real well.

Jesse: We need to cover this up a little bit more.

Abe: Jesse's strong as my brains. *[He laughs.]*

Ms. Woolf: You're as strong as Abe's brains? I don't know, Jesse, do you agree with that?

Jesse: Probably.

Ms. Woolf: Yeah, that's an excellent drawing. *[Ms. Woolf looks at the draft of the mask that lies next to the head and then looks at the papier mâché mask in progress.]* Uh huh. We can cut the mouth out too.

Abe: That's what we said.

Ms. Woolf: Yeah, but we have to wait until it's completely hard and then we'll cut it out.

Jesse: So we could actually do that instead of like try-
                ing to get lips on here and stuff? *[He points to
                the lips on the draft.]*

Ms. Woolf: Yeah, if you want those little lips, I think they
                would enhance it, and make it look a lot better.
                Just go ahead and do that roll like you've got.

Jesse: It is supposed to be like flames from the mouth.

Ms. Woolf: Well, just cut those out with an Exacto knife.
                *[Ms. Woolf leaves the two and moves on to help
                other students.]*

Ms. Woolf supported what Jesse and Abe had done and offered some technical advice on how to make parts of the mask more stable. These two students were confident in speaking about their artistic and technical decisions with their teacher, and did not feel that Ms. Woolf wanted to change their piece in any way. Rather, Ms. Woolf saw her role in this instance as a person who had the technical expertise in art to help these students make a stronger and better art piece. She regarded students' visual expressions as their own.

At the end of the term, many students, like Jesse and Abe, began to make their own decisions on what to omit or include in their representations. Their interests, as Kress (1997) suggested, continued to be an ongoing motivational force. Abe and Jesse made decisions about how to work within the semiotic system of art to represent the information they wanted to express in their papier mâché. They, in effect, became more competent in their knowledge of art and felt more independent. They did not rely on Ms. Woolf for her approval, but depended on each other for both artistic inspiration and technical support. Here, Abe and Jesse talk about their final decisions concerning the aesthetics of their mask:

Abe: How long are you going to make these? *[Refers
                to the wire and yarn hair]*

Jesse: I don't know. Hey, what about these horns? Are
                we going to paint them brown?

Abe:	I don't know. How about black?
Jesse:	I think, trust me, it's going to look better in brown. *[Referring to the yarn]* Maybe we can get some gel to make it stand up.
Abe:	Maybe we can paint a brown stripe down the middle.
Jesse:	*[To Peggy Albers]* How do we make the hair stand up?
Peggy:	How about wrapping it around pieces of wire?
Jesse:	*[To Abe]* We need to make the hair the same length.
Abe:	No, we don't. Hair's not the same length.

Jesse and Abe were completely at ease with the decisions they made concerning the construction and the aesthetics of their artworks. They had worked together to solve construction issues, asked for expert advice from Ms. Woolf, and learned from these experiences to become literate in art. They learned the limitations and the possibilities of the semiotic system to represent their ideas. They knew what tools and techniques are available to artists, and had received instruction in how to use the tools as well as artistic and technical support for their ideas.

Abe and Jesse represented the many students who found that freedom of expression was one of the most important things they learned in Ms. Woolf's art class. Testimonials from other students confirm this. As Amy wrote in her journal: "I've learned a lot here, I'm going to miss art. I think it was fun because in here we got to use are [*sic*] heads and think alot [*sic*]. We got to be creative. I think you teach wonderfully and I can't wait until next year!!" Tobi's entry agreed with Amy's: "I learned a lot about horizon lines. I have realy [*sic*] enjoyed art. I liked all of the drawings and all of the things that we did. I liked it and I am sure that the next class will like art two [*sic*]." These two students explicitly stated, they had enjoyed art, but more importantly, they had learned something from the teacher about art, form, and expression. Shane theorized her change of beliefs about herself as an artist, relating her development in technical skills to her concept of herself as an artist: "My believes [*sic*] have changed about art because I hated my art teacher last year. This year was awesome. My skills have also changed. I can draw better, and I can think about things to draw, paint, or sculpt easier now. Art was really enjoyable this year. I like art now!!!!!"

Recursive Reflections
and Constructive Conversations

Before their placement in Ms. Woolf's class, students had little experience in formally reflecting on their own learning. To encourage and support reflection, Ms. Woolf encouraged self-reflection on art in the form of artists' journals and ongoing conversation during the creation of artworks.

Artists' Journals

Ms. Woolf's strong support for the use of artists' journals in education came from her desire to awaken students to the process of art-making. As she said:

> We are beginning to learn more about the process that the artist thinks through. We are also exploring through their journals and diaries and their conversations with contemporaries about what goes on in their minds between the inception of the idea and the getting it down on paper. It's not just a one-way thing because you never crank out a masterpiece all at once.

In using artists' journals, Ms. Woolf found that her students' academic histories found their way into students' initial reactions to this idea. The following excerpt, which occurred when Ms. Woolf introduced journals to the class, illustrates the route Ms. Woolf took to navigate the problem of student affect toward journals:

> *Ms. Woolf:* We're going to start with something that I do in this class, journals. How many of you don't like journal writing? *[Nearly all raise their hands.]*

> *Ms. Woolf:* What didn't you like?

Ted: Writing.

Ms. Woolf: Why?

Mark: Bores me.

Candy: Takes too long.

Ann: It's not interesting.

Ms. Woolf: How many of you do not like journals because
                the questions the teacher asks are boring?
                [Nearly all raise their hands.]

Students initially resisted writing in journals largely because of their
unpleasant experiences with journals in other classes. For many, journals
were a waste of time because, as Abe said, "There's no use in doing journal writing. Why? So you can look at your writing when you're old and
say 'Oh, this is what I thought in art class'?" Others, like Curt, believed
that "Some days I don't want to tell the teachers what I feel." However,
Ms. Woolf explained that art journals would replace tests (to which the
students applauded), and would function as a way for her and her students
to negotiate grades. In addition, Ms. Woolf went on to distinguish an artist
journal from the journals most familiar to the students. She focused on
critique as a way for them to think about their own perceived growth in art.
In addition, she explained that these journals also function as ways to help
her become partners with them in the grading:

> I'm asking you to do a journal in this class, but it is not a daily journal
> that you write your feelings in. It is a critique journal in which you
> will reflect on your artworks and tell me what you thought you did
> well and what you would like to work on further. In this journal, you
> will be evaluating yourself. This gives you lots of power. . . . Let's
> say, you've just finished your first piece of your best artwork, for ex-
> ample, blue prints, landscapes, cartoons, models, and the like. . . .
> Evaluating is often arbitrary. What we do know is that you get better
> with art. I don't want to play God with your art. I don't know your art
> skills. I will look at your evaluation that you've written on your art
> piece.

This journal also will serve as a way for you and me to be partners in grading. In this journal you will write what grade you deserve and why. It becomes an argument in a sense that you argue that you deserve an "A" because you put in a lot of work. I'm also offering a spoken journal on cassette. For some students, their handwriting is not very legible and they get frustrated with writing. So, for those who would like to do their journal on cassette, you may. In this class you will get to explore what you want to explore in art. I may structure some of the format, but I want you to make sure that you get to learn what you are interested in.

On the first day of class, students created and wrote in their artist journals, which they made from six to eight sheets of unlined white paper folded in half and stapled in the middle. They illustrated their artist journals, identifying them in their own ways through colors, images, and language. After students had constructed their journals, Ms. Woolf directed their first writing assignment, in which students were to comment on their likes and dislikes, their past experiences, and the things they would like to learn.

The initial comments by the students were usually simple and short. Many of them wrote that they liked neither art nor their elementary teachers (see chapter 4), yet nearly all wanted to improve in some area of art. For example, Bill, who had encountered negative early experiences with art, wrote: "I want to become better at using a compass and protractor, and how to draw anything." Tori, whose experiences had been quite positive, wrote: " I want to draw better and become an artist." As noted earlier, Ms. Woolf used comments such as these to design a set of lessons that supported the skills students wanted to learn such as line technique, shading and drawing basic shapes, gesture drawing, figure drawing, painting technique, mixed media, 3-D wire, and clay and paper sculpture.

However, Ms. Woolf also wanted her students to move away from a view that art serves only to develop the emotional side of individuals (Collins, 1995). She worked to get students to think more critically about their work as they pursued the lesson goals:

Each time you do a critique, we'll look back at the example of the first artwork and see how your skills have improved. What we know through research is that art is like math and sports. The more you practice, the better you get. Compete with yourself. Journals help me know what your thoughts are about your work. It's never "dear diary" stuff. You will never have to do that.

As a consequence of her views, Ms. Woolf asked students to write critiques of their work after it was completed. As a framework, she provided the following questions to help guide their reflection:

1. Did you achieve your lesson goal?
2. Ask yourself if you like your artwork. (Does it feel like quality work?)
3. Ask yourself if there's anything you could do to improve your artwork. Ask your partner for his or her opinion, too.
4. What grade would you give your artwork? Why?

Initially, many of the sixth-grade students' reflections were merely restatements of these questions. For example, Noel wrote:

1. I feel I like I did everything in that lesson.
2. I feel like I could of did better.
3. Think before I write.
4. B+, because I feel like I did good and bad.

As students became more confident and comfortable in reflecting on their artworks, their responses became a bit more involved. For example, Ashley retraced her process in drawing a still life made of blocks:[2]

1. Yes, I guess I did. I tried hard enough; you can tell it is supposed to look realistic.
2. Well, it's okay, considering this was my first time drawing realistically.
3. I would redo shadows and show better gradation on my shadows. *[Ms. Woolf responds: Yes, excellent point. Also practice line and smudge technique and control lines and coloring strokes. (Shows this on cylinder)]*
4. Probably a B- because the gradation on my shadows could definitely be improved.

Ashley's articulation of what she has learned might not yet be as deep or clear as we might expect from an 11-year-old, but it demonstrates considerable movement in the short space of several weeks and indicates that she was learning to describe and reflect on her meaning-making processes in art. Ms. Woolf also contributed to the critique by suggesting ways in

which Ashley could improve, sharing techniques, critique, and a vocabulary to use in talking about artworks. By going back to pieces, thinking
about them, and articulating that thought, students produce an "audit trail"
(Harste & Vasquez, 1998) of their learning in which their attitudes and
accomplishments are chronicled as a token of the complex learnings that
have occurred in the studio art class.

Critical Conversation

Part of what contributed to the students' ability to begin the work of chroni-
cling their growth were the critical conversations they had with their peers
and Ms. Woolf. These conversations pushed them to dig beneath the activity level to the mental operations of each lesson goal. Of course, an obvious question is how students developed new ways of thinking within the
framework of subject matter with which many had encountered negative
experiences.

At the start of the term, Ms. Woolf found that students often were
hesitant to do artworks that were not completely prescribed by the teacher,
perhaps because of their previous experiences of prescriptive art education with its emphasis on getting the product right. To counteract these
feelings, on the first day of her classes Ms. Woolf assured students that
their ideas are important to how they grow as artists. She told them about the
importance of reflective critique, and the process of making art, explaining
how her curriculum would be different from their elementary art experience:

> If we talk about the importance of critique, it's a movement in and out
> of your mind. It is what you think, what you've experienced over a
> period of time, and between the production of each artwork as well.
> Then we try to take down all the barriers to success, one of them being
> that you do an artwork, you're done forever, it's graded, and that's the
> end of it. In my curriculum, at any time, you can redo or rework a
> piece of artwork for a regrade of that artwork as your skills develop-
> ment progresses. Because that's also available, there's another move-
> ment of that knowledge and problem solving that can go to another
> level. This can help you become successful and have another experi-
> ence over the top of a previous experience with that particular art
> production. So what I'm trying to get away from is art for art's sake in
> the sense of art education being production based.

This kind of talk was foreign to students. Initially, they could not believe that a teacher would offer them what Murray (1982) called "the ter-

rible freedom to learn" (p. 133). However, as the class progressed students began to realize that they could rework an artwork at anytime during the term to demonstrate what they were capable of doing rather than be graded on what they could not do.

Optimal learning occurred, though, when Ms. Woolf provided individual oral feedback in the context of the production of the student's representations. In these individual consultations, students were able to contextualize the group demonstration and apply the skills to their own artwork. In this individual consultation on figure drawing, Martha learned more about creating a more realistic figure from Ms. Woolf:

> *Ms. Woolf:* Just try to draw the basic shapes in figure drawing. Do you see the basic shapes there? This is the foot, but do you see how you have her legs and feet going? I would have her turn just a little bit. *[Ms. Woolf draws these shapes on Martha's paper.]* Then, bring her legs out. Then you can put her chair in there under her. Her chair would go in there like that. Does it look like she is sitting on it? Do you see it in there?

> *Martha:* Yeah, but how do you get shapes when they are not like circles?

> *Ms. Woolf:* Remember? You go like this. You look at her pant leg. She's got some wrinkles there. That comes down and then it goes up. Do you remember the demonstration on the board? And then you erase what you don't need. You might need a little bit better eraser. Do you see that it starts to look like a pant leg after you erase some of the lines?

> *Martha:* Um hm.

> *Ms. Woolf:* Okay. Then you can shade a little bit to get it to look like it's in shadows there. That's how you do it.

In this demonstration, Ms. Woolf engaged Martha in thinking actively about the visual text she was creating and in making these thoughts visible. This process involved a great deal of visualizing, imagining, selecting, and forming, work in which Martha needed to exercise both her eye and her hand, attending closely to detail. This process also involved a great deal of risk as other students observed and, in passing, evaluated her artwork.

In another example, Cathy was in the process of making a round-shaped piñata. As Cathy layered paper on her piece, Ms. Woolf helped her to think about the details of working with the rim of her papier mâché piece:

> *Cathy*: What should I do now?
>
> *Ms. Woolf*: Double check the rim, Cathy, and I say that because it cracks any place where the paper is too thin and there's not enough glue. Yeah, like right there where your fingers are. Any place where there is already a bit of a crack, it will open up like that on you, so smooth that around and then the very top of the bowl. Yeah do exactly what you are doing with your fingers and that will protect it from chipping and breaking.
>
> *Cathy*: Like this? *[Cathy smooths out the edge of her piece.]*
>
> *Ms. Woolf*: Okay, that's fine.
>
> *Cathy*: How long should I do this?
>
> *Ms. Woolf*: Keep layering until you have a nice thickness around the rim.

In this short dialogue, with the help of Ms. Woolf, Cathy organized her thoughts about how to strengthen her piñata, continued to compose her artwork, and created a form that she desired. Organizing, composing, and forming are central to making artworks. These acts can be facilitated when students are offered oral feedback in the context of their own artwork. Group demonstrations were good in getting Ms. Woolf's students started, but individual feedback enabled students to take larger risks, be open to alternative perspectives and ideas, and extend their imagination. This act of creating new images involved a lot of trial and error, of working and reworking pieces, moves that ultimately led toward student independence in their own artistic skills and abilities.

Critical conversations occurred not only in the context of artwork production, but also once artworks were completed. Ms. Woolf created exhibition opportunities similar to those of practicing artists. These exhibitions offered another type of feedback, that which arises from public arenas in and out of the classroom.

Ms. Woolf's students displayed their artworks not only in the classroom, but also in the showcases outside the library and art room, and on the hallway walls near the art room. In addition to these common public exhibits, Ms. Woolf organized an art show in conjunction with the spring musical concert. More than 100 students selected the artworks they wanted to exhibit and framed them for the show held at the Riverview High School. For many students, this public recognition was important in their growth as artists.

Community members often talked with Ms. Woolf during the art show and commented on how impressed they were with the talent of middle school students. During one of these art shows, Peggy sat down and talked with Jim, a student in Ms. Woolf's class, and Kristine, his mother. Unlike her son Jim who was often quiet during class, Kristine loved to talk. Jim was a talented cartoonist, but often was teased by many of the boys at school because of his interest in art. During this particular show, Jim had several pieces on exhibit along with a portfolio of his cartoons available for the public to see. Kristine talked about Jim's emotional struggles in this school and the importance that art played in helping him get through these middle school years:

> Jim and I have been in Riverview for about 15 years and are doing pretty well. I own a florist shop. Jim gets his artistic ability from his father; he's an architect. We're divorced now. Jim is always being teased in school. I don't know why, but I think it's because he likes art so much. Ms. Woolf has provided a sanctuary for him and really supports his art. He goes to her room all the time, and she gives him encouragement. Jim now sees himself as an artist because Ms. Woolf has given him so much good feedback.

Through the art show, students' talents, like Jim's, were made visible to the Riverview public. Students received feedback when a community member stopped and looked at their artwork, and made comments such as this: "I can't believe that a sixth grader could do that," or when they congratulated a young artist on his or her artwork, or, in their conversation with Ms. Woolf, complimented the young artists.

Freedom, form, and feedback were essential as students learned the limitations and possibilities of art. They began to know the tools and the grammar of art, how to represent meaning visually. They became free to explore the ideas that permeated their lives. However, in the representation of these meanings, student values and their underlying ideologies become visible. It is to these areas, the literate expressions students create and the messages these expressions offer, that we turn in the next chapter.

NOTES

[1] The number of lesson goals depended on the number of weeks Ms. Woolf taught the class. When she had six week classes, her students typically moved through eight lesson goals. When the class term was increased to nine weeks, students were able to move through nearly 12 lesson goals.

6

IDENTITY, IDEOLOGY, AND IMAGE

Ellie: Let me draw Richard.

Franny: I need to draw my dream lover.

Ellie: I have to draw Richard.

Franny: Does he have black hair?

Ellie: Probably brownish-black.

Franny: Everyone's gonna find out. I told some people.

Ellie and Franny's conversation, centered on the real and imagined boys in their lives, focuses our attention on an aspect of students' visual representation of meaning beyond that of their growing technical skills as artists and their desire to represent meaning. Their artworks and the contexts in which the artworks are created provide reminders of the ideologies underpinning and permeating these artworks as expressed by their sign-makers.

As students talk with one another, interacting as learners, collaborators, teachers, and critics, they are engaged in literate acts. An exploration of the ideologies underlying their literate acts, their sign-making, permits us to infer something of the messages signified, even when these messages may not be immediately transparent in the artworks themselves. Such an exploration asks us to consider questions such as this: What values underlie the artworks created at RMS? How do these artworks reflect the ideological contexts in which they were created? What do these artworks say about the representational desires of students at Riverview? What is the literacy represented in student artworks?

Racializing Colors:
Whiteness, Blackness, and Art

As previously described (see chapter 4), the students at RMS live not just in a community where the identity of racial Whiteness is the norm. In Riverview and at RMS, the racially White "phantom center" is more than a place in which "the dominant discourse tries never to speak its own name" (Ferguson, 1990, p. 11), a place where the structures of society have evolved so that Whiteness is rewarded and other racial identities are marginalized. Riverview and RMS are also places where acts of intolerance and marginalization are acted out at the individual (as well as the systemic) level, where verbal and physical aggression against non-Whites are not merely overlooked but sometimes supported through the words and actions of members of the town.

Several episodes in art class indicate that the views of the community were all too quick to become the views of the students at RMS. For instance, in the spring of 1995, Ms. Woolf overheard three eighth-grade boys talking about how they had been to the Ku Klux Klan (KKK) rally at the state capitol. As Ms. Woolf reported:

> They talked about this as if they were going to an amusement park.
> This bigotry and sort of thinking is really hard for me to deal with.
> With my being [a Cherokee and lesbian], I find the atmosphere much
> more repressive and suffocating. It's very hard to hear about these
> sorts of things [the KKK rally].

Inevitably, attitudes such as these were expressed in the artworks of Ms. Woolf's sixth-grade students. For instance, Stan and his partner Craig were two boys who did not wholly engage with art, did minimal work on their artworks, and tended to find other distractions to occupy their time in this class. After Ms. Woolf had completed a minilesson on how to release bubbles in clay to avoid explosion in the kiln during firing, Stan grabbed some chocolate-colored clay and a wooden cylinder used to roll clay into slabs. Looking at Craig, he grabbed the cylinder, and raising it over his right shoulder, beat the clay, calling out, "Rodney King, Rodney King."[1] Several other boys mimicked Stan's actions as they engaged in the process of creating their own individual artworks. Such behavior might be passed off as an aberration, an episode of boys trying to gain the attention of other boys by engaging in outlandish behavior, were it not for other incidents of this type and the larger context of racial bigotry that permeated the school and community.

Such was the acceptance of bigotry that it inevitably found its expression in the artworks of individual students. For instance, in one of Ms. Woolf's classes, a papier mâché work being created by Lane piqued Peggy's interest. From afar, the artwork seemed to be shaped as a large cone. It looked like a mountain of raw and unpainted paper. As Peggy went closer to look at it, she noticed that Lane had carved eyes out of this unfinished artwork. She stopped to talk with its artist, Lane, a sixth-grade boy:

Peggy: Hi Lane. What are you making?

Lane: A mask.

Peggy: How did you think of this idea?

Lane: I saw it in a book and thought it was cool. I just
             wanted to make one.

Although Lane's description of his artwork as a "mask" was minimal, within this community and this part of the state, this artwork only could be a KKK mask. The idea that Lane, a sixth-grade boy who could be characterized as quiet and diligent, represented his beliefs in this way demonstrated his understandings concerning the depth of acceptance accorded the sociocultural values in which he was immersed. When Peggy talked with Ms. Woolf about such artworks, Ms. Woolf theorized as follows:

> Art creates a natural tension between the reader and the artist through the artwork. The artwork itself visually identifies the belief systems that the artist holds, while at the same time, the readers of the artwork interpret the artwork through their own belief systems. The artist doesn't find his or her representation offensive, but has chosen to make a statement about his or her beliefs. However, sometimes the artist may not be conscious of what ideologies she or he is presenting in his or her artworks.

Because the context of the generation of Lane's work is known, it is possible to situate the work in the belief systems of Lane's community. Interestingly, readings of Lane's artwork other than a reading of racial intolerance are possible. For instance, it could be imagined that a mask of this type was created to critique, to resist the very meanings the context permits to be read. The absence of a face behind the mask could be read as a critique of the faceless other often associated with the KKK. But the context of its production reveals the ideologically driven hatred that underscores Lane's work. Lane's artwork, like any other representational effort that works against the human dignity of others, "*initiates* rather than closes off the problem of responsibility. That is, it requires that one hold open for assessment those practices which generate one's claim to knowledge" (Simon, 1992, p. 16, emphasis in the original).[2]

Images such as Lane's demonstrate that art does not merely draw on the aesthetic and affective nature of humans. Rather, it makes visible the ideologies from which students represent meaning, ideologies that may be disconcerting and quite troubling. A graphic rendering of the extent to which extreme racism could go was present in the work of another student. Barry, also working with papier mâché, constructed a nearly life-size papier mâché figure of an African American male (see Figs. 3.37 and 3.38, chapter 3).

Barry used what he knew about form and representation in three-dimensional (3-D) format, as well as the media of papier mâché and paint to create an image that was provocative on several levels. He created an image of an African American person, but the overwhelming element dominating the piece was that of mutilation and degradation. As is somewhat evident in Fig. 3.38, the figure (standing about 4 feet tall) has no arms: Instead, blood-red paint marks the sockets where arms should be. The figure has a red slash across the throat and, in a jarring representational move, the figure is depicted with a smile painted on its face.

Again, as with any artwork, multiple readings of Barry's sculpture are possible, one of which is a critique of the very objectification and degradation represented. The smile on the face of the figure can be read as a sort of defiance in the face of the physical torments that have been wreaked on the body of the figure. However, this would be the reading of a liberal interpretivist. In the context of Barry's sociocultural milieu, another reading is a much more likely reflection of the meanings signified by the artist. This reading subjugates the African American. The sculpture not only dehumanizes the figure, but reduces the figure to a state lower than most life forms because the figure depicted does not seem to have the sense to realize its own tortured state or its own pain. Ultimately, Barry, as a White artist in a community infused with racial bigotry, signals his White superiority in this sculpture.

Notably, the racism exhibited in the conversation and sign-making of the students at Riverview was located among the boys in Ms. Woolf's classes. This pattern raises questions: Is artwork itself somehow instrumental in bringing racism to the fore? If so, why? For example, Barry's artwork may be an example not of a release of the imagination (Greene, 1995) made possible by art, but its retrenchment into stereotypicality, an enactment of the fear of discovering that a subject area such as art, which is often identified as feminine, might reveal a lack in these adolescent boys—the lack of machismo. Barry's and Lane's artworks and Chris's beating of clay and chanting "Rodney King" may suggest that boys turn art, a feminine-identified subject area, into something fused with aggression and other behaviors that they think are "more acceptable" for males. We explore this element of gender differences in attitudes toward art and in artistic representation as we examine the issue of gender and art in Ms. Woolf's classroom.

Gender's Representational Roots and Routes: Boys and Girls Doing Art

The racial and gender attitudes exhibited by some of the students in Ms. Woolf's classroom echo those outlined in the description of their community presented in chapter 4. These roots of prejudice and bigotry permeate the community and become the sources of inspiration for artistic representations. However, as suggested by some of the work in the previous section, other roots affect the representational routes that Ms. Woolf's students take up in their work. As their bodies are maturing physically, preteens and teenagers become focused on sexuality and their gendered identities (Belenky, Clichy, Goldberger, & Tarule, 1986; Miedzian, 1991; Thorne, 1993). Given this pattern, it seems logical that their preoccupations and curiosities find expression in interactions around artwork and in the productions of artwork. In particular, the students of Ms. Woolf's art classes revealed their gendered selves when they talked with each other in the context of art class, when they talked with their teacher and Peggy about the artwork of well-known artists and through the artworks they themselves produced.[3]

Gendered Talk in Art Class

Relationships in art class began the first day of class when girls and boys
picked partners. Girls always chose to work with other girls, whereas boys
always chose to work either alone or with other boys.[4] In an enactment of
Gilligan's (1990) warning that "adolescence seems a watershed in female
development, a time when girls are in danger of drowning or disappear-
ing" (p. 10), the girls at RMS subverted their own individuality to foster
good relationships. In doing so, they also reduced the chance of ridicule or
exposure.

In the excerpt that follows, Tracy, Carla, and Alexa carefully negoti-
ated their artistic identities using strategies all too commonly associated
with the subjugation of identity in females. Through self-abnegation and
carefully positioned commentary on personal skill, the girls' conversation
suggests that the establishment of their interpersonal relationship is more
important than the recognition of achievement of some type of standing in
art.

Tracy:	What are you going to make?
Carla:	I don't know. I'm not very good at drawing art.
Tracy:	I'm not either.
Alexa:	I'm going to draw some hearts.
Tracy:	I'm just good at drawing people, not things.
Carla:	*[Leaning back in her chair and looking at her paper]* I don't know what to draw.
Tracy:	I'm going to draw a person.
Carla:	I think that I'm going to draw a dog.
Tracy:	You're good at drawing dogs. *[She talks to Carla.]* Here, turn your face. I need to see the shape. *[She physically moves Carla's face to a profile position.]*

The girls continue to demonstrate their desire for the maintenance and importance of the interpersonal by encouraging the efforts of each other.

Tracy: I better draw the person better. *[She thinks about this idea for a minute or so.]* I'll draw a little girl with a ponytail. *[She mimes tying her hair back into this hairstyle.]*

Alexa: *[Shows her finished drawing of a house]* Tracy, I'm done.

Tracy: That's good.

Peggy: Are you drawing someone in this room, or are you creating her in your head?

Tracy: Someone in my head. This is what I used to draw when I was a young artist.

Carla: I just don't know what to draw.

Tracy: *[To Peggy]* She's good at drawing puppies.

Alexa: Why don't you draw a puppy dog? *[She moves to the counter where there are photocopies of animal shapes. She gives one of these photocopies to Carla.]* Draw a dog.

As some of the girls came to realize that Ms. Woolf's classroom supported both their need for relationships and valued their skills as artists,[5] they began to learn that they could express their knowledge about art and art skills openly and without risk of embarrassment or self-consciousness. Alexa, for instance, did not hesitate to show her drawing to Tracy or Carla. She was confident that her artwork represented what she intended and looked to her partners for comment. Even though Carla had not decided on a subject matter, both Alexa's and Tracy's comments seemed to spur her on to drawing.

As the girls worked within supportive relationships and learned to critique their content in healthy ways, they gained confidence in critiquing each other's work later in the term:

Artie: Is there anything I can do to make this better?

Monica: Maybe a little shadow over there.

Artie: I did. I'm going to say in my critique that I drew
                 all the shapes, and shaded them. *[To Monica]*
                 Do you see anything wrong with this?

Monica: No.

Artie: And, I'm also going to say *[Referring to the con-
                 tent of his journal critique]* that Monica didn't
                 see nothing wrong with it.

Ultimately, then, the girls worked to maintain relationships as they
worked to produce art. They focused on the task at hand, the production of
artwork, not as an opportunity to outperform or undermine their peers, but
as an opportunity to extend and build a supportive set of relationships in
which individuals were valued for their particular expertise.

Boys, too, found their sense of identity in relationships, but these relationships looked quite different. Instead of desiring a connectedness that
worked with and through the tasks in which they were engaged, boys often
talked about matters other than artwork or school.

*[Peggy sits with two boys working on their drawings and
talking about the standardized test scores that just came out.
These scores are deciding factors as to whether they have to
attend summer school.]*

Stan: Arty sent out some stuff for summer.

Rick: I already sent out for summer school stuff.

Peggy: Do you have to go to summer school?

Rick: I think so. My mom's gonna get me 'cause of
                 my grades. If I bring my grades up, end of mid-
                 term, I might not have to go.

Like girls, boys enjoyed socializing with their partners about matters other than school. Yet, unlike the girls, within these relationships, there was not an overt discussion supporting the agenda of creating of a quality piece of art. Rather than talk through ways to improve their art, oftentimes they talked socially about the artwork as it related to their interests:

Jeremiah: The Pacers are doing pretty good.

Ezra: If they win tonight, they go to the playoffs.

Peggy: Who are they playing tonight?

Jeremiah: The Knicks.

The boys' tendency was to work independently even when partnered. Collaborative relationships focusing on the production of artwork, like those of Abe and Jesse who collaborated on several artworks, or those of Carl and Adam who worked on a wire sculpture of a car, were far fewer among boys than the collaborations among the girls.

Many of the boys operated with the belief that the work they produced was "good enough" for the class.[6] In essence, either they felt that they controlled the techniques being taught and had completed assignments satisfactorily or they still were being dismissive of the seriousness of art as a field of study. In general, boys often took less time to complete their assignments than girls. Some boys used the time after writing their journal critiques to disturb others who were working. Unlike the girls, who expressed uncertainty or offered suggestions to their partners, boys were less likely to talk about their artworks in terms of making their pieces better. They often just explained what they were doing:

Peggy: How are your pieces coming along?

Jerod: I'm still wrapping mine. I'm going to papier mâché tomorrow.

Chester: I still have to make the head.

Jerod: So do I.

Chester: Mine's the Headless Horseman.

Jerod: I'm making an Indian Headdress.

Neither Jerod or Chester talked to each other about how to make their artworks better. Their talk in art class was on social matters, not on their representational efforts. The boys worked independently and without discussion about improvement in their artworks.[7] Drawing from the work of Sadker and Sadker (1994), it would seem that the boys' beliefs about their own capabilities in accomplishing specific tasks meant that there was little need for others to tell them how to do their work.

This reticence to engage in critique, perhaps read by boys as an exercise in self-deprecation, led them rarely to critique their work in any depth in their journals. Several weeks into the quarter on their self-evaluations, the boys were not hesitant to give themselves A's, which they justified by saying they liked their work instead of framing a more substantive response. When asked how they might improve their work, they rarely submitted an in-depth answer. Noel's journal critique is representative of many responses from the boys:[8]

Lesson Goal 1: Create an example of your best artwork.

Q: *Did you think you achieved the lesson goal? Explain.*
A: I feel like I did everything in that lesson.

Q: *Do you like your artwork? Explain.*
A: I feel like I could of did better.

Q: *How could you improve your work?*
A: Think before I write.

Q: *What grade do you think you deserve? Why?*
A: B+ because I feel like I did good and bad.

Lesson Goal 2: Create a blind contour of the class.

Q: *Did you think you achieved the lesson goal? Explain.*
A: I achieved the lesson goal.

Q: *Do you like your artwork? Explain.*
A: Yes, because it is funny.

Q: *How could you improve your work?*
A: Keep trying not to look up.

Q: *What grade do you think you deserve? Why?*
A: B. I think I did pretty good.

Lesson Goal 3: Learning perspective (depth/space). Compose a landscape drawing showing depth, using a horizon line and at least one magazine image (cut out neatly). Be sure that the size of your image suits its placement in the foreground, middle ground, and/or background. Style may be realistic, surrealistic, or fantasy. Use color.

Q: *Did you think you achieved the lesson goal? Explain.*
A: Yes.

Q: *Do you like your artwork? Explain.*
A: Yes because I like monster trucks.

Q: *How could you improve your work?*
A: Make more scenery.

Q: *What grade do you think you deserve? Why?*
A: A+ because I did everything.

During week one, it seemed that Noel wanted to reflect on his work, but his experience in writing reflective journals appeared to be limited. He believed that his artwork was pretty good so he gave himself only a B+. He showed confidence even in his first week of class, accomplishing everything in the lesson goal. By week three, Noel took little time to reflect on his work, and even though he believed he needed to add more scenery, he gave himself an A+. He seemed to believe that because he did everything, he deserved an A. This sense of self-esteem and confidence in their ability was more evident in the boys' than in the girls' work.

The few boys who engaged with art worked a great deal on detail, but this changed as they grew older. For instance, Nick, a sixth-grade boy, spent a great amount of time with each pencil or colored drawing that he did. His artwork showed that he spent a great deal of time working through a lesson goal, such as the one on proportion, composition, and gradation. He kept a portfolio of work that he showed at the annual art show, and often won first prize for his drawings. Because Nick liked art, some of the boys in his grade often called him "gay."[9] By the time Nick advanced to eighth grade, he assumed a more aggressive role in art class, one that resembled, in part, other eighth-grade boys' aggressive behavior.[10] He often did not work on his art pieces during class, moved around the room aimlessly, and disturbed the girls as they worked.

In general, although the boys engaged in conversations about their artworks, they tended to focus less on how to make their artworks better and more on their interests and the subject matter of the artworks. If they were intrigued with a technique, they worked with it for a long time. Abe and Jesse, discussed earlier, talked a great deal about drafting, techniques, and constructions of artworks. They were more the exception than the rule in terms of talking through the process of constructing visual representations.

The boys and girls in Ms. Woolf's class appeared to bring to art classic stereotypical ways of interacting—girls with their focus on relationships and boys with their focus on activities such as sports, girls who subjugated their own identities as blossoming artists to maintain relationships with their peers and boys who assumed the sufficiency of their artworks and seemed to exercise care in not being too identified with the feminine subject of art. There were exceptions to these patterns, such as Nick. However, these exceptions often proved the power of the peer culture in the school. Overall, the gendered interactional patterns provided some insight into how the students were constructing their gendered identities, and set the context for considering students' perceptions and constructions of artistic representations.

Engendering Renderings

As part of her art curriculum, Ms. Woolf created opportunities for students to think explicitly about their beliefs regarding identity and art. In one such engagement, students were asked to predict the gender of an artist (if they could) based on photographic prints of 16 artworks completed by various artists. A range of media was used by the artists, and all of the artists' names were covered.

Nearly all the students predicted the artists' gender incorrectly. Typically, students predicted that an artist who composed images of family life, serene and pastoral scenes, and interiors would be female, whereas artists who composed images showing blood and violence, created massive sculptures, or worked with highly technical drawing (as in Maurits Esher's work) would be male. The following conversational excerpt is illustrative:

Yancy: I thought only men would do the horses, the large sculptures.

Alison: I thought the flowers, the ones with the flowers would have been done by women.

Yancy: I thought that, too.

Charlie: I saw an artist, it was on spring break. I saw that he liked to draw flowers.

Ms. Woolf: Did that seem odd to you at the time, that he did the flowers?

Charlie: No.

Ms. Woolf: Well, that's good.

Anthony: I judged the pictures by the colors.

Ms. Woolf: What colors did you think women would use?

Damek: Soft, soft colors, really.

Charlie: Bright colors.

Ms. Woolf: Why did you think that? Can you take this one step further into your brain and say why you thought that?

Johnny: The pictures that showed blood, the bloody stuff,
              is more rougher. And women are made of sugar
              and sweet stuff.

Larry: That's a real sexist comment. Some girls aren't
              like that.

Alison: I think that the reason some people are sexist is
              because they think of only certain people, and
              not all of them.

Carrie: You think of girls wearing pink colors, purples.

Alison: And like baby clothes, most of the clothes for
              boys is blue.

This conversation demonstrates that these students constructed gender in very concrete ways, drawing, as Gilbert and Taylor (1991) suggested, on the media and popular culture, among other things. Young girls often construct images that situate them in a "culture of femininity" (Christian-Smith, 1990). Carrie and Alison, for instance, have worked with their ideas about the kinds of images that female artists *ought* to construct, and may have drawn on stereotypical notions of femininity, for example, that females learn to "speak softly or not at all; . . . to value neatness and quiet" (Sadker & Sadker, 1994, p. 13).

Similarly, the fact that Yancy, Anthony, and Damek believed that male artists are associated with blood, violence, and massive images suggests that school knowledge and community and popular culture images show males as inherently violent and aggressive. This again draws on the stereotypical image that boys are, by nature, aggressive (Gurian, cited in Kantrowitz & Kalb, 1998).

Having a gendered identity that is fixed or inscribed into social relations would appear, on the face of it, to make life simple for these teenagers. However, such superficial simplicity is deceptive. Teenagers are daily faced with the question that Walkerdine (1990) posed: "What is the struggle which results from the attempt to be or live a unitary identity?" (p. 103). Some of the struggles consonant with the living of unitary gendered identities were revealed during a conversation with a different group of students in Ms. Woolf's class as they responded to their perceptions about the identity of the artists for the pictures they were viewing:

Ms. Woolf: Why do you think the artist is a male?

Carl: It's a picture of a girl naked, and a girl wouldn't draw herself.

Ms. Woolf: What if she was in an art class and the model was female?

Frank: She's a pervert.

Pete: She'd turn her head.

Carl: Only males would draw naked ladies.

Alan: I'd put clothes on her if they gave me a naked lady to draw.

Pete: I'd put clothes on it. If it was a male and I had to put my name on the bottom *[Referring to the signature on the drawing]*, they'd think "He's gay."

Ms. Woolf: Let's explore that. Pete, you said if a male drew another male, others would think he was gay.

Pete: People would think he was.

Carl: If a male drew a man, he would be looking at his private parts.

Ryan: If a male drew another male, he might not be gay, but if he drew a naked male, he would be.

Pete: Either that or he'd probably be gay if he drew a male and thought "Hey, you're sexy" and stuff like that. I think he'd be gay if he drew him naked.

Ryan:	If he did draw a naked male and he wasn't gay, either he used to be a woman and had a sex change or he's messed up in the head.
Carl:	He wouldn't be gay if it was like his grandson.
Several male voices in unison:	Oh, yeah, he would!
Ryan:	Hey, Grandpa! Have a look at this! *[He points to his crotch.]*
Ms. Woolf:	If a woman drew another woman, would you say she is gay?
Several male voices blend:	Only if she was naked.
Ms. Woolf:	If you were in an art class and your grade depended on drawing a nude, what would you do?
Pete:	You'd flunk.
Alan:	I'd draw a naked girl but not a naked boy.

In this discussion, Carl, Pete, Alan, Ryan, and Frank announced their identification with all "normal" males, those who are heterosexual and, by definition, antigay. Their open identification with heterosexuality offered them safety from any identification with gays and the desire to look at nude males. To be a male artist and draw male nude models defined the male artist as gay, and "messed up in the head." Rather than jeopardize their identification as heterosexuals, these young adolescent males would rather flunk than draw a male nude model. On the other hand, to be a male artist and draw a female model was normal because men and women naturally fell into a heterosexual relationship, and this was the accepted ideological position in this school and community.[11]

This identification with "straightness" is not unusual. Britzman (1995) suggested that schooling is all about teaching "straight." Indeed, the manner in which the RMS students read the artistic texts they viewed is similar to the reading practices in many schools. These reading practices are characterized by "exorbitant normality," in which "'the other' is rendered either as unintelligible or as intelligible only as a special event, never every day. Exorbitant normality is built when the other is situated as a site of deviancy and disease, and hence in need of containment" (Britzman, 1998, p. 85).[12]

These conversations among students about artists and their artworks supplement the data on the interactional patterns of the students in Ms. Woolf's art classes. They suggest the strength of the normativity at RMS and foreshadow the elements likely to be found in students' representations in Ms. Woolf's art class.

Gender Signs

In the artworks they produced, the students of Ms. Woolf's Riverview classes inscribed their gendered identities in terms of the content of their artworks and the media used to create the artworks.

Choice of Subject Matter. Overall, when girls portrayed females in their artworks, they located those females in the domestic sphere, in romantic relationships with males. The focus of these artworks was that of the private sphere or the home. The artworks of females also conveyed a sense of self in relation to peers and to spirituality. For boys, the subject matter of their artworks focused on their interest in cars, sports, music, hunting, and weapons such as guns, sabers, knives, and swords. Boys often indicated a sense of self in relation to the public realm, independence, and superiority.[13]

Melissa's artwork seen in Fig. 3.20 (chapter 3) is representative of many artworks created by adolescent girls. In this image, Melissa represented a strong theme that runs through females' artworks, a sense of self in relation to family. This image may be read as Melissa's rendering of an idealized past or future. In this image, Melissa fulfilled the stereotyped understanding of what constitutes femininity as predicted by adolescents earlier in their discussion of sexism. For her drawing in Fig. 3.20, Melissa used a "soft soft color" palette in her representation of the balloons, the clowns, and the mountainous backdrop. Melissa's "sweet stuff" theme underpins the artworks of many other females in Louise's class.

When boys constructed femininity (and this was not often), they positioned themselves as namers of what constitutes beauty in women. They saw themselves as more powerful because they are what adolescent girls desire. They, therefore, can name who is beautiful to them or what constitutes a woman who might be their chosen mate. Boys' representations contrasted in that when they depicted females, they depicted them as objects of beauty or victims to be rescued. One popular rendering was that of the "damsel in distress."

Girls more often than boys constructed artworks that depicted heterosexual relationships (real or imagined) with boys. As the artworks in Figs. 3.18 and 3.27 (chapter 3) suggest, girls seemed more willing to forego their own individual identity to identify themselves with a boy.

Along with their desire to be in a relationship with boys, girls often indicated their sense of self in relation to spirituality. According to Piper (1994), girls during adolescence actively search for meaning and order within the universe. Some girls become very religious and represent themselves in relation to God. Candy's wire sculpture of a crucified Christ (see Fig. 3.1, chapter 3) and Serena's very spiritual drawing of Christ's hands folded in prayer visually demonstrated their allegiance to a Christian way of knowing. In this strongly religious community, this is not unusual. In addition to portraying identity through religion, girls also become environmentalists or advocates for the poor or sick (Piper, 1994). Samie drew a sketch of herself as a doctor, whereas Krista created a children's picture book about her training of a dolphin.

In nearly all cases, boys created artworks in which they viewed the dominion of males as outside the home. They positioned males as hard public laborers who enjoyed leisure outdoor activities such as hunting, fishing, and golfing. In their artworks, Pete saw himself as a golfer (see Fig. 3.19, chapter 3), Matt viewed himself as a professional race car driver (see Fig. 3.17). Others saw themselves hunting (see Figs. 3.3 and 3.4) or as spectators of professional basketball (Fig. 3.13) or baseball.

Sadker and Sadker (1994) argued that by being placed in starring roles in school, boys seem to hold onto a gendered identity that resides in a past that girls are learning to question. This emphasis on heroism appears to lead boys to a rich fantasy life as imagined in their artworks, in which males are depicted as mighty medieval warriors, racing car stars, or experts in martial and armament arts.

Choice of Media. The comments made by students about their perceptions concerning the work of other artists did and did not predict the choices
they made as they produced their artworks.

On the whole, girls seemed to demonstrate a preference for working
with drawing and painting (see Figs. 3.14, 3.18, 3.20, 3.22, 3.25, and, 3.26,
chapter 3). Many were very deliberate in learning to shade, devise perspective, and create an illusion of depth. They also engaged well with clay
sculpture (see Figs. 3.23 and 3.39), better than with wire, wood, or both.
They tended to spend time creating subject matter that would be appealing
to others, mostly mothers and fathers and siblings. When it came to working with wire, girls tended to create artworks that were 2-D (see Fig. 3.12)
rather than 3-D (see Fig. 3.1). They created flat images of flowers (see Fig.
3.12), hearts, and initials of their favorite boy. Lydia's creation of a 3-D
hat on which she mounted a daisy after painting it yellow and Candy's
creation of a 3-D figure of a crucified Christ (see Fig. 3.1) were atypical of
the works produced by girls using wire.

Some of the girls' resistance to creating a greater number of 3-D pieces
might be explained by Sadker and Sadker (1994), who suggested that girls'
inexperience in working large may contribute to their reluctance. However, when given the challenge and opportunity, and when working with
particular kinds of materials, the girls in Ms. Woolf's class demonstrated
their competence (see Figs. 3.15 and 3.16, chapter 3). When working in
paper, for example, girls collaborated to create table-size sculptures such
as a sunflower created by Alice and Mary. Furthermore, in their own pre-
dictions about what female artists do, girls and boys did not associate wire
sculpture or large sculpture with females. Overall, though, girls tended to
choose painting and drawing over sculpture when they worked on extra
credit projects.

Boys preferred to work with sculpture and technical drawing (see Fig
3.33, chapter 3) rather than paint scenes or engage in nontechnical drawing. In particular, boys chose wood, paper (see Figs. 3.2, 3.6, 3.7, 3.10,
3.11, 3.37 and 3.38), and wire (see Fig. 3.36) sculpture over clay sculpture. Boys often worked large and, on occasion, some worked
collaboratively to create huge artworks that spanned the width and length
of two black-topped tables (approximately 6 by 8 feet). In several instances,
boys collaborated to create a large papier mâché mountain that ended up
being a volcano. Abe and Jesse worked on a large mask (see Figs. 3.5, 3.6,
and 3.7), and Ted created a 5-foot Micky Mouse.

In general, the students enjoyed experimenting with the movement
and mixing of different colored acrylic paints on paper. Carmine and Faris

spent nearly 30 minutes pouring red, yellow, white, and blue acrylic paint onto a canvas, moving the paint around on the paper, and observing how some colors remained distinct whereas others blended to create different shades. Many students, both boys and girls, chose to play with color design by taking various colors and letting the paint drip from the small plastic containers onto paper canvases. The students then folded the canvases in half to see the symmetric design that was created. Others painted the table surface, created a design on the table, then pressed the paper to the table to see the reverse imprint made from monoprinting.

In addition to creating these images, the girls and boys often were deliberate in their choice of colors. The girls most often chose softer hues, such as pinks, yellows and light blues, whereas the boys used stronger hues, such as blacks, browns, and purples. Yet, two girls, working collaboratively, moved into darker shades:

> *[Kirsten and Emma are working on a collaborative artwork in which they move from painting shapes to layering dark colors over their initial subject matter.]*
>
> *Peggy*:   Why did you move from shapes to dark colors?
>
> *Kirsten*:   They are happy colors.
>
> *Emma*:   See? *[She places blue drops of paint onto the paper canvas, which Kirsten then paints into the already thickly painted surface.]*

Although dark colors are not commonly associated with happiness, these girls interpreted dark blue as depicting happiness, thus creating their own definitions of the meanings of colors despite being taught color theory and having it readily accessible through its posting on the bulletin board. Others talked about how colors influenced their meaning making:

> *Brooke:*   Art is a lot of things. Like this piece. I was in a
>   sad mood. If you look at her, she seems sad. Her
>   eyes make her sad. I didn't use bright colors to
>   make her look happy. I used dark colors.
>
> *Patty:*   Colors express mood.

> *Brooke:*   Blue does this. *[She points to a powder blue sky
>   and her deeper blue for the ocean.]* It depends
>   on what kind of person she is. Some people even
>   wear darker colors even when you're happy.

For example, one girl created a yin and yang symbol using black and white (see Fig. 3.29, chapter 3). Another girl used bright dark reds and blues to represent her favorite sports team. Like girls, boys frequently chose colors that are more commonly associated with their gender. They often chose bright but dark colors, and liked to work with darker hues such as browns, blacks, dark purples, and reds. They rarely chose to work with pastel palettes.

Literacy Intersections: Identity, Ideology, and Image

The social interactions that occurred during sign-making and the meanings that can be read from student artworks (signs) suggest a complex view of literacy at work. This view does not portray literacy as the acquisition of a set of skills, but presents literacy within a much larger framework. This view of literacy echoes the social semiotic views of Kress (1997), in which sign-makers work within a semiotic potential: "the resources available to a specific individual in a specific social context" (p. 8). This view of literacy also draws on the work of Barton and Hamilton (1997), which portrays literacy as social practice.

In both chapter 5 and this chapter, we worked through the dual concepts of art as literacy by examining the development of emerging control over the media used in artwork and the meanings produced through the use of that media. We recognize that because the artworks discussed were produced within the domain of school, they represent specific kinds of practices—bounded by "doing art" in the context of school, limited by the carved-up time fragments permitted by school, mediated by notions of the substance or lack of substance of art as a subject matter, and so on. These are not the vernacular practices of art—the art of the streets, the art enacted as part of being a member of a society in which visual culture permeates everyday life from the shopping bags used as luncheon sacks to the insignias on jeans or sneakers to the images in magazines or on postage stamps. Yet, the artistic literacy engagements of the students in Ms. Woolf's classes are replete with the personal and the social. Like all literacy practices, the artistic engagements of Ms. Woolf and her students are "embedded in broader social goals and cultural practices" and are "historically situated"(Barton & Hamilton, 1997, p. 7).

The community of Riverview and RMS are communities marked by racist and homophobic perspectives. That these perspectives permeate the ways in which students construct and represent their identities and those of others should not come as any surprise. When students draw on KKK hoods or exorbitant heterosexual normativity, they are drawing not merely from their immediate context but from the history of belonging in Riverview, a history that has shaped "what it means to belong" to such an extent that discourses on overt racism, sexism, and homophobia are tolerated by school officials.

If there is a surprise in the art classes of Ms. Woolf, the surprise is not that Ms. Woolf found herself, both personally and ideologically, assaulted by the Riverview identity as it was acted out in interpersonal interactions and in works of art.[14] Rather, the surprise is that art, as a form of literate expression, took hold despite its low prestige status in the school and despite its association as a feminine form of expression.

The art biographies of the RMS students told of art teachers who knew little about art and artworks, castigation by their teachers, or awareness that they were uninformed by any technical knowledge and longed for something else. Their prior experiences, however, would have led them to the likely hypothesis that they were to experience a repeated litany of the lost opportunities of their elementary school years. Even though some boys enacted their fear of art (through disruptive behavior), by and large, most students worked to produce works of art that demonstrated an emerging awareness of technique, an ability to select and work with a variety of media, and a willingness to include experimentation as part of learning. These lessons were more than lessons in the technical skills of working to create literate images. They were the beginnings of a shift in the ideological position of artistic literacy practices in these students' lives. This shift began to occur because the processes of production were demystified and because students were active participants in thinking and talking about art.

Ms. Woolf was a singular agent of difference at RMS who had many levels of difference to confront. Despite the marginalization of art within the school, students were seduced by the power of sign-making that it offered. Although it is true that Ms. Woolf may have been troubled by the images produced in her class and the ideologies that undergirded them, there is no doubt that her students experienced a range of opportunities to create visual texts that they had not thought possible based on their other experiences with art. Given this state of affairs, two questions seem to loom large: How might art in elementary schools be organized so as to open up an even greater range of meaning-making possibilities for students than those experienced by the students in Ms. Woolf's classes? How might all meaning-making activities work to explore issues concerning the content of representations so that issues of human dignity are injected into classroom discourse? We offer some beginning exploration of possible answers to these questions in the last chapter.

NOTES

[1] The reference to Rodney King relates to the 1991 beating of Rodney King, an African American, by four Los Angeles Police Department officers. A videotape of the beating aired on national television. When on April 29, 1992, only one of the four officers was found guilty of the use of excessive force and the other three officers were cleared, riots began to break out across Los Angeles and continued for about 3 days (The Los Angeles Riots, 1992).

[2] Ms. Woolf struggled to open up the question of responsibility, even though she, like others (Rosenblatt, 1938; Steiner, 1995), holds to a view concerning the openness of the interpretation of text, to the idea that the meanings of a text/artwork occur as a result of the transaction between the text and the reader. Ms. Woolf repeatedly attempted to help her students see themselves in a non-Riverview world, a world filled with a multiplicity of racial, and gendered identities. As she said on one occasion:

> I don't allow harassment speech to go on, the hate-speech. I call them on their use of the word "nigger" and "faggot" and try to explain to them that someday they will get out into a community, perhaps larger than Riverview, and they're going to want to have another understanding of how those words function than the ones they've grown up with.

[3] Bruner (1996) argued that artworks should be viewed not as final products, but as ongoing artifacts of thinking. By capturing the interactional patterns of the students in Ms. Woolf's class, we complement our inferences about the patterns in student artworks with evidence of the values that inform their thinking. We begin our exploration of gender and art by examining the nature of the relationships that the students in Ms. Woolf's class have as they work to create art.

[4] In some classrooms at Riverview, like the classrooms that Dewey (1911) commented on some 80 years ago, girls are often placed with boys to keep the boys from acting out. For many girls, working with boys is problematic because "they talk about weird stuff":

Peggy:	What do you mean by 'weird stuff?'
Genevieve:	Fighting.
Patsy:	Stupid stuff.
Peggy:	Why do you think they do so?
Genevieve:	They are weird.

Although the girls did not articulate further what they meant by "weird" or "stupid," what they meant comes through in how boys addressed girls, the ways in which they teased girls, and the ways in which they talked pejoratively about girls' capabilities:

Linny:	I just don't like how this school doesn't let girls on the football team. I want to try out for the team.
Chuck:	*[From across the room]* Girls can't play football.
Beth:	Yes, we can. You're just afraid.
Linny:	Yes, we can. We can probably do better than you. You are afraid that we will do better.

[Chuck and his partner (male) laugh.]

[5]   With knowledge about the work of feminist scholars such as Brown and Gilligan (1992), Fausto-Sterling (1985), and Walkerdine (1990), and literacy scholars such as Harste, Short, and Burke (1988) and Goodman (1994), Ms. Woolf was consciously aware of the need for girls to establish relationships, engage in supportive and critical conversations, and provide an environment that encouraged "habits of the mind" (Dewey, 1938). Brown and Gilligan (1992) argued that establishing strong relationships for girls in adolescence is "crucial for girls' development. . . and also for bringing women's voices fully into the world" (p. 7).

[6]   One explanation for this response may be that at the middle grade level, nearly 48% of boys feel "capable of 'doing things'" compared with only 29% of girls (Sadker & Sadker, 1994, p. 79). The Sadkers argued that part of the difference in self-esteem derives from males' confidence in their athletic ability and girls' general expectation that adults do not believe that girls will do well. In the current study, this capability for males might be regarded as an overconfidence in their understanding of what is expected and what is deemed adequate performance by them.

[7]   Jesse and Abe, profiled in chapter 5, were an exception to this pattern.

[8]   Ms. Woolf provided a set of guiding questions to help students structure their journal writing. She worked through illustrative examples of the types of responses that helped students and her to reflect on art. Consequently, although the questions could be answered in a fairly limited manner, in actual fact Ms. Woolf had schooled students to respond to them much more particularly than the face value of the questions might suggest.

[9]   Collins (1995) discussed the widespread belief that art develops only the emotional and "feminine" side of learners. Many of the boys in Ms. Woolf's class associated art with feminine characteristics and extended this association to stereotypical views of gay males.

[10]   One possible explanation for Nick's change in behavior could have been a desire on his part to make sure his peers recognized him as heterosexual, as one of the crowd. Consequently, his expressions had to be overt and the kind that would convince others of his masculinity. To not adopt these behaviors would have meant that Nick would have needed to endure name calling and other types of harassment.

[11]   This view of the female model, as Collins and Sandell (1984) suggested, is understandable. The number of female images in Western art (and reinforced in advertising, commercial illustrations, and other forms of popular culture) show females as "passive, available, possessable, [and] powerless" (p. 30). Males come to know females as "attractive objects" rather than "active, effective doers" (Collins & Sandell, 1984, p. 31).

[12]   Ms. Woolf understood the need to disrupt the normative dialogue and did so through conversation. However, she did so with some trepidation given the PTA's strong belief that homosexuality was irrelevant in their schools, and the community's strong evangelical beliefs that positioned homosexuality (as well as her own lesbian identity) as wrong or deviant. Her worries are transparently articulated in the following excerpt:

And as you know from the one school board meeting, there are a lot of parents in this community who don't want us to teach QUEST classes that deal with no put-downs. They don't want us to teach kids not to put one another down. They don't want us to say anything positive about gays. I think that I hold them [students] accountable for things that they say. I walk a tightrope there when I tell them that that's abusive and they shouldn't use those words. And I'm afraid that, at times, it's interpreted that a homosexual is a bad thing to be, and that's why I don't want them yelling that to one another. That's an area that I feel uncomfortable with because I don't feel that way at all. I've gone as far as to challenge students with, "How many homosexuals do you know?" "Do you think that's a logical basis/judgment to make, that a faggot is a terrible thing?" I often get, "Well, my pastor says it" or "My mom and dad say it," and then I just don't touch it. I know I walk a tightrope there.

[13] The descriptions of student artworks echo, to some extent, those of Lindstrom (1957), who commented, for students in the 8- to 12-year-old range:

The girls have certain notions of feminine beauty. . . . the men [boys of this age] draw are usually 'rough-tough' types. . . . Domestic life has no interest as a theme for most boys; action and adventure and criminal ferosity predominate if human beings appear at all in their pictures. (pp. 63–64)

[14] In this climate of intolerance, Ms. Woolf often handled homophobic or racist incidents on a one-to-one basis, as exemplified in the following excerpt:

Margie:	I don't know if I could be friends with her. My parents might get mad. My dad is so afraid that I will be like my aunt who is gay. We go to the mall and he will say, "Margie, there is a nice looking man.", as if I am going turn out that way.
Kay:	Ms. Woolf, do you think that you could be friends with a girl who has both a boyfriend and a girlfriend?
Ms. Woolf:	Yes, I could. I have many friends who are gay.
Margie:	I think that I would like to have a relationship with a girl, but not until I'm older.

Ms. Woolf attempted to confront racism, sexism, and homophobia as much as was possible. However, with very little faculty support toward this aim, her individual efforts were minimized by the sheer amount of accepted intolerance.

7

CREATING CONDITIONS
FOR ART AS LITERACY

The social history of art shows. . . that it is accidental that certain types of artefact are constituted as "art." (Wolff, 1993, p. 14)

We admire child art for its expressive directness and its ability to communicate an emotion to a wide range of viewers. But aren't these characterizing traits of child art also qualities for which we praise the great paintings in museums. Yet no aspect of modern art has elicited more anger from its defenders and its alienated viewers alike than the sense that it looks in some way like what children do. (Fineberg, 1997, p. 21)

Children, unlike most of their teachers and parents, are comfortable using virtually all of the expressive modalities. (Gallas, 1991, p. 21)

The three domains of human culture—science, art, and life—gain unity only in the individual person who integrates them into his own unity. (Bakhtin, 1990, p.1)

Art, and children's art in particular, is fraught with dilemmas. What is art? Who makes art? What is the role of education in the making of art? To whom is art answerable? Ms. Woolf's sixth-grade classes were a particular enactment of answers to these questions. Using her class as a starting point, we explore the ways in which education can create the condi-

tions to expand the conceptualization of art in schools. We also consider the obligations a person enters into by engaging in representation.

Art: Definitions that Create Possibility

Questions about the nature of art have long been debated (Berland, Straw, & Tomas, 1996; Davies, 1991; Paley, 1995; Staniszewski, 1995; Thompson, 1990; Wolff, 1993). From the optimistic stance of Greene (1995) who argued that "art offers life; it offers hope; it offers the prospect of discovery; it offers light" (p. 133) to the perspective of Wolff (1993) as quoted earlier, who challenges what artifacts can be considered art, the nature of art has been interpreted in numerous ways. Part of the work that Louise Woolf did in her classroom was to open up the definition of art. She accomplished this opening up in several ways.

At a simple level, the inclusion of materials such as wire for sculpture, in addition to the traditional school materials of paper, paint, and scissors, meant that the student art makers in her classroom had a greater range of representational possibilities open to them. However, at more complex levels, Ms. Woolf's classroom offered much more.

Louise Woolf worked with multiple layers of art as literacy and, in doing so, began the work of demystifying art. She had her students undertake art criticism and explore art history by looking at "high art," the works of the masters. These works were available through books and slides. But she attempted to move her students beyond looking to interpretation, pushing them to consider who might have painted a picture and why they might think so.

Ms. Woolf reminded her students of "vernacular" art—the art of T-shirts, tennis shoes, and other artifacts of popular culture. She can be seen as taking seriously the challenge of the postmodern era to break down "categories such as art, popular culture, domestic product, and media" (Tickle 1996a, p. 18) and to expand the conceptualization of art to embrace art in its fulsomeness. As some student comments revealed, this idea of vernacular art stuck with them, perhaps niggling at and beginning the work of dethroning the more traditional perspective of art as high culture, as something separate from the pursuits of ordinary people.

Finally, Ms. Woolf challenged students to reconstitute their concepts of their own artistic abilities. One of the times she explicitly did this was in her discussion of figure drawing, but observations in her classroom indicate that she repeatedly assumed that her students were art makers, and in doing so, she instilled in students a hope and, for some a realization, that they were artists. She seemed to accomplish this through following some of the same principles we used to describe emergent artistry in chapter 2:

- She assumed her students would be intentional about their art making.

- She assumed her students would decide when their works were "enough" to do the representational work they intended.

- She allowed for experimentation and hypothesis testing as well as the possibility of her students extending their knowledge or acquiring self-confidence in their skills by choosing to work with a specific medium or content they had used previously.

In a way, then, Louise Woolf invited her students to reclaim their openness to representational possibility—the openness described by Gallas (1991) and Fineberg (1997) as being characteristic of younger children, an openness that had been eradicated, at least in part, by school practices in relation to art. This reclamation project worked not only to reformulate the way in which "the institution of the school has given knowledge a bad reputation" (Rollins & K.O.S., 1995, p. 43), but also worked to reformulate what art might mean as a representational system.

Ms. Woolf's stance toward art is a departure from the activity-based programs characteristic of many schools (Collins, 1995; Eisner, 1997). Collins (1995) argued that such programs emerge primarily because of the belief that art is a feminine-identified subject area. Identified as such, instruction in art yields a number of problems. Art often is viewed as an "enrichment" subject and therefore frequently relegated to late Friday afternoons, or as a "treat" for good behavior. Other subject area teachers "feel free to ask art teachers to adjust their art lesson plans to correlate with what is being studied in these subjects" (Collins, 1995, p. 48) while not entertaining reciprocal requests. In these activity-based programs, literacy in art is often confined to cutting, pasting, and coloring.

Because feminine qualities are ascribed to art, its value is often seen to lie in its "ability to provide for the catharsis and articulation of emotion" (Collins, 1995, p. 48). As a consequence, students with severe behavioral problems are assigned to arts-based classes (especially drama and art) to "release tension, experience success, and increase and reclaim their self-esteem" (Collins, 1995, p. 48).

Art's identification as "women's work" also may result in art instruction in which the artworks created primarily serve decorative purposes instead of being concerned with larger representational questions. Especially in elementary schools, art is focused around nationally celebrated holidays such as Halloween, Thanksgiving, and Valentine's Day.

Attitudes that diminish art are difficult to eradicate and probably represent decades worth of work. Nevertheless, Ms. Woolf's perspectives on art exemplify one example of a point of departure for educators considering how to embrace art as literacy. Ms. Woolf's views on art teaching present a challenge and raise classic questions in art education. Specifically, Ms. Wolf approached art education with the belief that art should be taught by artist educators using a studio approach. We examine the issues related to these beliefs, interspersing examples of art education in other settings and trying to come to terms with alternatives for those who find themselves working in conditions beyond their control.

The Studio Approach

The studio approach used by Ms. Woolf highlighted a method of teaching in which the "*locus of control* [is] away from the teacher. . . and towards each student in the class" (Clark, 1994, p.88). In this type of approach, as described by Clark (1994) and which is in keeping with many principles of emergent artistry outlined earlier, students are in charge of resolving artistic choices. The boldness of a line, the color, and the emphasis or focus in the design all are choices of the student art makers themselves. Students, when uncertain, can move about the studio space engaging in investigations of materials or conversations with others that will complement or extend their perspective on the issue confronting them. The teacher's role is more like that of a parent, who must gradually reduce the degree of intervention, assuming that children will become more independent as they handle increasingly more difficult tasks.

Assumptions Underlying a Studio Approach

Underlying the general description of the studio approach are several assumptions that may make it less feasible in some contexts. The first of these assumptions is that of structured time and space dedicated to art. Even though Ms. Woolf's working conditions were less than ideal, she was at least in the position of having art timetabled into the school's curriculum. Many schools do not even make this gesture.

Time for Art. As both Eisner (1997) and Mimms and Lankford (1995) suggested, one of the factors adversely affecting art education is the scant amount of school time that is devoted to teaching art. According to Eisner (1997), time is an "absolutely necessary condition for the conduct of any field of study" (p. 28). However, the amount of time allocated for art in elementary classrooms is abysmally minute. Eisner (1997) calculated that in grades 1 through 6, less than one half hour per week is devoted to the teaching of art. This, he states, amounts to less than three percent of school time per week.

At the secondary level, only 15% enroll in art, and 85% of students do not study art at all. In many high schools, art is more likely to be offered as an elective than as a course required for graduation or college entrance (Collins, 1995; Eisner 1997). Part of this is explained by the way in which education is affected by standardized tests (Murphy, Shannon, Johnston, & Hansen, 1998). Media messages focussed on dropping scores, inadequate teachers, and illiterate high school graduates pressure schools to focus more attention and time on subject areas that are tested rather than carve out more time for art instruction.

Mimms and Lankford's (1995) investigation into art education found that a typical elementary art teacher is female, spends 48 minutes a day setting up and preparing materials for student use, and has one 50-minute period per week to teach art to several hundred students. Time spent in classrooms on art instruction is inadequate, and if children are to more fully develop art skills and gain confidence in their own visual constructions of meaning, art educators argue that students must spend more time with art.

A solution to this perspective is to embrace our broad conceptualization of art as a social semiotic system used to represent meaning. Such an understanding invites less segregation of representational systems, especially at the elementary school level where the social practice of carving up the disciplines is only partially entrenched. If classrooms were envisioned as places of inquiry, not unlike the art studio, perhaps as knowledge-making studios, then more opportunities for using a variety of semiotic systems to represent meaning and interpret the varied representational efforts of others would be possible. If students and teachers were made aware of themselves as inquirers, as meaning makers, as persons engaged in constructing and reconstructing realities with those around them, then it might become clear that reality is multiperspectival, always open to new constructions and interpretations (Greene, 1995).

Of course, as Clark (1994) reminds us, the positioning of art as one of the vehicles through which education occurs must guard against the positioning of art as being of secondary value and "the mis-teaching of artistic and aesthetic activities by non-specialist educators" (p. 96). For instance, unless carefully implemented, the teaching of art as part of integrated themes can result in a greater degree of ownership by the teacher, repetitious engagements, and a sidestepping of interrogating art as a historical and contemporary form of representation.[1]

Material Support for Art. Although Ms. Woolf found support lacking for some aspects of her art curriculum, for the most part, students were provided a variety of materials with which to work. In addition, there was storage space and a sink for use. These seem to be key essentials in any art program, whether studio based or classroom based. However, because of the low status attributed to art in the curricula of many schools, the money, materials, and space allocated to teachers for art instruction are, at best, modest (Collins, 1995; Eisner, 1997; Mimms & Lankford, 1995).

Mimms and Lankford (1995) found that on the average, schools spend $3.33 per student on art materials. Some teachers have reported being given only 20 cents per student compared with others who were given $20. Moreover, the typical teacher often spends her own money to supplement her budget, and also feels undervalued in schools where art is not considered a serious subject. Collins (1995) argued that because art is considered enrichment, when "monies for space, equipment, personnel, and materials are divided, art teachers are less likely than those who teach basic subjects to get what they need to maintain a quality program" (p. 47). Although teachers attempt to find space for art materials including clay, papier mâché, paints, and tools used with these media, most teachers find the obstacles too overwhelming.

Many teachers are without a source of water, storage space for children's artworks, or the time it takes to tidy up their rooms properly (clean rooms being a priority for many schools) (Eisner, 1997). This results in teachers generating art projects that are clean and require few materials, thus reinforcing the desire to engage children in art projects that demand only cutting, pasting, and coloring skills, and severely constraining representational possibilities in art.

Although recent documents on literacy (NCTE Elementary Section Steering Committee, 1996; NCTE/IRA, 1996) support the development of visual literacy, it remains to be seen whether such efforts translate into fiscal support for the arts in classrooms. Nevertheless, such initiatives represent a beginning.

Artist Educators. For Ms. Woolf, a further assumption underlying the success of any art program is that those who educate in the arts should themselves be artists. As indicated in chapter 4, she felt that her burgeoning development as an artist in her elementary school years could have been bolstered by teachers who knew the right questions to ask or the demonstrations of technique that were needed. Some, such as Clark (1994), suggest that the studio approach can be used by generalist or specialist teachers as long as they are operating within their "thresholds of security" (p. 90) as the locus of control shifts from teacher to student.[2] However, Clark (1994) went on to suggest that the teacher–student trust necessary to create the kinds of conditions supportive of studio experiences occurs in an inverse relationship to familiarity with school. That is, in high school, where students and teachers meet for only short periods, trusting relationships are difficult to develop because of the constraints of the timetabled, fragmented organization of the high school curriculum, whereas at the primary school level where a single teacher works with a class for the entire day, trusting relationships are more easily developed.

Whatever the case, it appears that in most elementary classrooms in the United States, art is taught by generalist teachers who are insufficiently prepared to teach art. Because many teacher education programs require few, if any, art classes, elementary teachers often rely solely on their own art experiences, which, for many, ended with junior high school. Moreover, many "know little about the arts and often trivialize them in their classrooms" (Eisner, 1995, p. 9).

At the elementary level, relatively little instructional time is devoted to art instruction. When classroom teachers are required to teach all subjects including art, they often schedule art on Friday afternoons rather than during prime instructional time (Collins, 1995).

To further complicate the matter of art instruction at the elementary level, the number of trained art educators working in schools has grown increasingly smaller through the years. Eisner (1997) offered his own state as a case in point. In 1967, there were 408 art supervisors or consultants in 1,000 school districts in California. Today, there are fewer than 50.

In essence, the possibility of engaging artists who also are educators is another long-term goal for art education in the public schools. Such a goal requires a continual pressing for the agenda of art education in the schools. Some inroads toward this end may be made through the framing of art education, both theoretically and pragmatically, as part of the larger work of being literate in a contemporary society that demands visual and print literacy. To inform the process of conceptualizing possible paths to enhancing art education, we depart from Ms. Woolf's context to consider options that have been explored in other contexts.

Other Options in Use

Among the options for developing literacy in art that we examined were those that involved artist educators, those that involved generalists, and those that involved some element of in-service education in art education. Some of these options were classroom based and others field work based. We suspect that part of what makes any of these options work in any particular context is the stance toward the literacy of art that is taken in the school and community, as well as the pedagogical perspectives adopted by the teacher.

Discipline–Based Art Education. We begin our exploration of art options by considering Discipline–Based Art Education (DBAE). Through DBAE, students are schooled in four areas: art criticism, art history, production, and aesthetics. The DBAE approach represents one attempt to elevate the status of art in school curricula.

In the early 1980s, the rhetoric of concern for excellence in education directed public attention to such publications as *A Nation at Risk* and *High School: A Report on Secondary Education in the America* (Efland, 1990). In response to the challenge of excellence, Discipline–Based Arts Education, coined by W. Dwaine Greer, emerged as a major influence on art education in 1984 (Efland, 1990). Developed by Manuel Barkan, Elliot Eisner, Ralph Smith, and Harry Broudy, DBAE is an approach to art education that, in Eisner's (1990) words,

> ought to engage youngsters in the making of art, it ought to help them learn how to see visual qualities in both art and the environment, it ought to help them understand something about the relationship of art to culture over time, and it ought to engage them in conversations about the nature of art itself. (p. 424)

More specifically, DBAE forwards four components of art that the "founding fathers of DBAE" believed build excellence in art: art history, art criticism, aesthetics, and production. In a very short time, DBAE "caught and held the attention of the art education field as a whole, in a way that was unprecedented" (MacGregor, 1997, p. 1).

Funded by The Getty Center for Education in the Arts (often called "The Getty"), DBAE met with both praise and criticism. For some, the implementation of DBAE meant that art was finally considered a legitimate part of the curriculum. A number of developments in art instruction emerged such as prepared materials useful at different levels, games and vocabulary cards, added historical information in textbooks, and games to design time lines and place artworks in a geographic context (Greer, 1993).

The DBAE approach was designed to shift responsibility from the art specialist to the classroom teacher, and to justify the art curriculum by theoretical considerations derived from aesthetics, art history, and art criticism (Broudy, 1990). Both arts education specialists and classroom teachers were disturbed by the DBAE project, especially the classroom teacher who was likely to be "uneasy teaching art without the talent for making art" (Broudy, 1990, p. 433). Classroom teachers, however, have found DBAE to be a good framework within which to teach art. For example, McNeal (1997) designed and implemented the first fine arts program ever offered at the university level in the western Arctic. She found that "building in DBAE principles and disciplines. . . . opened the students' eyes to their own cultural histories, and to the histories of other cultures in the region" (p. 82).

Even though DBAE has seen a rapid acceptance in the field of art education, a number of art educators have critiqued the intentions of The Getty for viewing "art education as the study of past cultural achievements certified by credentialed experts" (Efland, 1990, p. 254). Viewed in this way, Efland (1990) contended, art learning becomes a passive form of engagement, as demonstrated through the reduction in the importance of studio studies.

Several key criticisms emerge from DBAE. Arnstine (1990) argued that DBAE misses a major function of the arts "to acquaint the young with the culture in which they live" (p. 417). The focus of DBAE on masterpieces of fine art in Western culture is "likely to turn students away from the culture in which they live" (p. 417) and denies that the arts are "directly expressive of the culture in which students live" (p. 418). Arnstine believed that although students should study masterpieces, they should not do so until they are ready, when they can "genuinely enjoy them." Jagodzinski (1997) forwarded an often articulated criticism that, by nature of its wealth and position to influence large numbers of people, The Getty disregards artworks created by non–White artists. Collins and Sandell (1984) argued along similar lines by asserting that more attention to feminism within DBAE is warranted.

An interesting aspect of these debates is that the time calculated to be spent on any of the four disciplines in elementary classrooms is minimal. Mimms and Lankford (1995) stated that an average elementary art teacher spends 29 hours per year teaching art. In these 29 hours, 19 hours are spent in studio production, 4.5 hours on art history, 3 hours on art criticism, and 2.5 hours on aesthetics. As a consequence, elementary teachers are given little time to work with their students' evolving literacy in art, especially in studio production.

With such meager time allowances for students to immerse themselves in art, it is no surprise that students begin to peripheralize art very early. They learn very little about the tools and ways to express meaning visually. Good art comes to mean a very particular kind of art. Finally, the students learn that art lies outside their own lives.

The Reggio Emilia Approach. The field of early childhood education is the site of another approach to art education. The city of Reggio Emilia in Northern Italy near Milan has become known for its approach to early childhood education. This progressive and prosperous city of 130,000 has, only since 1993, captured the attention of American educators who travel to witness Reggio Emilia's emergent literacy program.

Having begun after World War II, the Reggio municipal early childhood system consists of 22 preprimary schools for children 3 to 6 years of age and 13 infant-toddler centers for children up to age 3 years (Davilla & Koenig, 1998). According to Davilla and Koenig, Reggio education is a communal activity, a sharing of culture explored jointly by children and adults.

Working within a pleasing environment, the Reggio approach views the teacher as a guide to gauge what the children know. Artists may work in the classroom alongside teachers who are knowledgeable about the arts and who are attentive to creating the conditions for children to use the languages of drawing, painting, clay, or wire to express what they understand. In essence, the children in Reggio classes explore a range of semiotic systems as representational devices. As their teacher studies the children's artwork, the process of documentation enables the teacher to understand the children's learning. The teacher and the children take the artworks seriously, using them for further discussion and educational growth.

Instead of viewing art as a discipline, Reggio teachers see art as a language by which children can express understanding of their environment, and the art studio becomes a place of research into what children understand (Davilla & Koenig, 1998). Furthermore, Schiller (1995) argued that children "do indeed understand the concept of graphic symbolic representation and can be expected to use it in a more sophisticated manner" (p. 47). For Reggio teachers, art is one of many semiotic systems through which meaning can be expressed. In the teachers' view, their role involves listening, reviewing, observing, and recording children's work as well as providing engagements that "facilitate the leap to the next level of understanding" (Davilla & Koenig, 1998, p. 19). Children sense that the teachers value their ideas and their work.

The Reggio approach offers much to study. Not only does this approach place art within a range of representational systems, but it also opens up questions about methodologies in teaching and the role of teacher observation and documentation in relation to learning. The relative newness of this approach to North Americans means that much more can be learned by an in-depth study of this context and the cultural translation of this approach to the North American context.

Art Curriculum Reform in England and Wales. In England and Wales, in an echo of DBAE, national legislation recently required that primary school teachers not only undertake practical art but also "perceptual, historical, and critical studies in art" (Tickle 1996b, p. 13). These activities are framed in two strands: (a) investigating and making, and (b) knowledge and understanding. However, room for interpretation was left in the curriculum. Tickle (1996a) describes the goal for 5- to 7- year-olds in the first strand (investigating and making) as "*experimentation* with materials, tools, and techniques in drawing, painting, printmaking and sculpture," whereas the goal for 7- to 11-year-olds is "to develop towards *control*" of materials, tools, and techniques. Lessons for 5- to 7-year-olds in the second strand (knowledge and understanding) "are to include introductions to the works of art in their locality, both from the past and contemporary work, and. . . from a variety of periods and cultures. . . [and] genres and styles" (Tickle, 1996a, p. 24), whereas 7- to 11-year-old children "are expected to extend their knowledge of art available to them in the locality by being able to identify the materials and methods used by artists" (Tickle, 1996a, p. 24).

What is interesting about Tickle's (1996b) description of the initiatives in England and Wales is that they involve generalist teachers who developed an action research agenda in relation to the demands of the revised art curriculum. Besides developing their own familiarity with art objects, local artists, the cultures informing the production of art, and the strategies used in art making, the teachers plan for students' engagements and their research into those engagements. The action research described involved developing relationships among the school, university, and community. The dozen teachers who each write a chapter about their action research projects relating to art education present a possible model for the broadening of artistic knowledge among teachers who are not artists. Part of their experience involves them, alongside their students, in learning to read or interpret artworks as cultural artifacts. Although the experiences are in relation to a local collection of art, the descriptions the teachers provide of their experiences and the experiences of their students indicate the potential of action research for developing an awareness of the breadth of art.

Art Reforms in Singapore and New Zealand. As in the Reggio schools, art education in Singapore has seen significant growth as recently as 1987 in the status of the arts in schools. Once thought of as peripheral to other subject areas and often taught after school or on Saturdays, the arts are now considered by the Singapore Economic Committee as essential to developing the "whole person" if Singapore is to educate students so that "they may reach their maximum potential and also cultivate a creative and thinking society" (Chong, 1998, p. 23). According to Chong, the arts curriculum in schools is taken seriously, as Singapore has a vision to be a "Global City for the Arts."

To complement the existing arts curriculum, which develops children's technical, aesthetic, and critical art skills from primary to secondary levels, the National Arts Council (NAC) implemented the Arts in Education program. This program brings performers to schools to expose students to different art forms and also takes students to live arts performance events. Although extracurricular, the Arts in Education program has seen enormous growth from involvement of 30,000 students in 1993 to 220,000 students in 1996 (Chong, 1998). Singapore, as Chong stated, is "embracing new challenges to support a growing arts scene" (Chong, 1998, p. 26).

In a similar vein, New Zealand saw the status and scope of arts education increase during the 1990s. Art now is an essential element of the contemporary school curriculum (Lees, 1998, p. 17). According to Lees (1998), several important factors led to this increase. First, there was an ennobling of the original Maori people, whose culture and knowledge were previously not honored nor considered worthy of representation in New Zealand's curriculum. New Zealand recognized the value of Maori's knowledge for its "relation to life, land, and religious and social ties, and for the contribution it makes to the well-being of others and to the expression of identity for its people" (Lees, 1998, p. 17). As a result, the arts were identified as one of the essential learning areas in the *Curriculum Framework*, formally acknowledging all aspects of the arts and culture as a distinct and valuable field.

The position of the arts as one of seven essential learning areas also has given a new level of support to performing and craft-based arts. Lees

(1998) stated that some ambiguity exists at the tertiary level, where the classical arts are being isolated within the university setting and not integrated into the "so-called seamless organization" of the university framework (p. 21). Inasmuch as increased importance placed on the arts has taken place rapidly, Lees (1998) asserted that New Zealand must "settle down," and arts education "must consolidate its gains, iron out the flaws, and become sure of its direction" (p. 21).

Although Ms. Woolf's studio orientation toward art offers her students a wealth of possibilities, in the short term, it is likely that, unless there is drastic change in support for art, this option will be viable for only a small proportion of classrooms. Besides garnering support for the shift in public and school-based sentiment that must occur, physical facilities need to be changed, financial resources reallocated, and time devoted to the education of artist educators. In the meanwhile, options such as those in England and Wales hold out some promise as teacher–researcher models for generalist teachers working toward developing both their own and their students' understandings of art. In addition, educational initiatives that reflect the role of art as one of many semiotic systems hold out hope for broadening generalist and specialist teachers' understanding of the possibilities of art as a form of literacy in the schools.[3]

The Art of Literacy: Questions of Responsibility

With an increasing number of educators[4] asserting that literacy, in today's world, is not merely confined to print literacy, schools must widen their definition of what counts as literacy. Catterall (1998b), for instance, argued that the arts are "great potential partners in academic learning, especially when we consider the general role of representation in how we learn and how we express our understandings" (p. 9).

If schools take the challenge to open up literacy, they must work with the dilemmas that such opening up entails. What is the result when the values of the meaning maker are at odds with the teacher's values? If the ideologies informing the creation of artworks (or any text) are intolerable, how is this intolerance spoken about, and how are students and teachers positioned in such a discussion. Is there a time when the silencing of representational efforts is acceptable? To whom is art answerable?

All of these questions are questions of responsibility and obligation. They are the questions that must be asked continuously, not of artwork in particular, but of all sociocultural possibilities, whether they be representational or interpersonal. As we illustrated in our examination of student artworks in chapter 6, even though we can infer the intention of art makers by listening to them and considering the pattern of their works in relation to the immediate and broader contexts of their production, artworks themselves can be interpreted in quite varying ways.

The power of any artwork or text lies in the meaning potential (Halliday, 1978) it holds for its art makers and readers or viewers. The background knowledge of readers or viewers has an inevitable influence on interpretation (Fehr, 1994).[5] For Ms. Woolf's students, racial and gender stereotypes that pervaded the community appeared to influence strongly, not merely the representations that the students created, but the interactions students had with each other in the art room. For Ms. Woolf, the degree to which she felt she could intervene in questioning the values of the larger community seemed to relate, in part, to her own sense of reading how far she could challenge without jeopardizing her employment and her status as a teacher in the school.

The decisions Ms. Woolf had to make were difficult ones. In deciding to make public reference to her Cherokee ancestry, she became the target of derisive and prejudicial comments. Informed by this reaction and the general climate of the school, she realized that she could never be open about her sexuality. However, her efforts to make students rethink their stereotypical assumptions about the artists and their artwork represented a significant step toward getting students to rethink the status quo.

Intergraphicality

Ms. Woolf used artwork to shift student sensibilities about art and gender. Although she did not articulate it as such, Ms. Woolf used the concept of intergraphicality (Freedman, 1994) to begin the process of making this shift. Freedman (1994) draws on Kristeva's work with "intertextuality" to demonstrate how people can develop an understanding of a new text by connecting it to texts they have encountered previously. From this perspective, no text rests in isolation. Instead, a text is always viewed in relation with other texts. Intergraphicality, which is similar to intertextuality, is "at work when images cue references to and cognitively integrate these images with others, building a network of imagery and meaning" (Freedman, 1994, p. 162).

Given their context, it is no surprise that Ms. Woolf's students identified particular colors and art media with specific genders. Simply by questioning students about their assumptions, Ms. Woolf began the process of asking them to think about the assumptions they held about art and artists. Of course, Ms. Woolf's interventions also included her daily work in presenting and referencing artworks that worked against these assumptions, even though the presentations may not have been announced as interventions. Indeed, Ms. Woolf's provision of these artworks provided additional visual texts for students to reference, thereby making the intergraphical relationships constructed by students more complex. However, Ms. Woolf's efforts paled in comparison with the press of the school and community values that surrounded her students all their lives.

Given art's marginalization as a subject area, Ms. Woolf's concerns related to being open about being a lesbian, her role as a woman teaching a feminine-identified subject area, and her Cherokee background, Ms. Woolf faced a multiplicity of difficult engagements in terms of challenging her students, her colleagues, and the school to be answerable to others about their beliefs. She chose her battles carefully with a view to making inroads. She seemed to be working from a position of hope. "Hope," Roger Simon (1992) said, "is the acknowledgment of more openness in a situation than the situation easily reveals" (p. 3). Hope allows teachers such as Ms. Woolf to enrich, broaden, and recognize the complexity of art as literacy, in spite of those who nominally recognize the influence of the arts in literacy learning (Geller, 1999).

Participatory Centered Education. Ms. Woolf's hope extended beyond the presentation of artworks the students might not have seen previously to include her discussion of those artworks, especially in relation to gender. Greene (1995) supported the need for students to engage in lively discussions about interpretations because "to get students' imagination moving in response to a text. . . may well be to confront the students with a demand to choose in a fundamental way, to choose between a desire for harmony along with an easy answer and a commitment to the search for alternative perspectives" (p. 129). In addition, Ms. Woolf offered her students considerable choice in their art making, an element missing from a community and school that had inscribed a narrow range of social understandings onto the youth of the community.

Such efforts go some ways toward the development of a "participatory-centered pedagogy that is not child-centered nor is it teacher-centered [but]. . . it focuses on building a community in the classroom. . . [and] place[s] respect at the heart of talk and understanding texts" (Murphy, 1995, p. 19). Participatory pedagogy arises from the work of scholars like Simon (1992) and Goodman (1992). This approach takes students beyond a recounting of their experiences in relation to classrooms, but asks them to be answerable for their discussion through critical reflection. As Roger Simon (1992) argued in relation to the creation of a pedagogy of possibility:

> Such a pedagogy will require forms of teaching and learning linked to the goal of educating students to take risks, to struggle with on-going relations of power, to critically appropriate forms of knowledge that exist outside their immediate experience, and to envisage versions of a work that is 'not yet'—in order to be able to alter the grounds upon which life is lived. (p. 57)

If Ms. Woolf could have spent more than a few weeks with students, her discussions with them could have focused on issues such as how people have come to associate colors or media with specific genders and why these associations have been perpetuated. These discussions, as foreshadowed in the excerpts we have presented, would not be easy discussions nor would they result in conversionary experiences. Instead, they represent the establishment of a site for a struggle to determine what knowledge is, how it gets constituted, and by whom. This struggle in itself can create a sense of community that asks participants to be answerable to each other not by virtue of superimposing one view over another, but by continually pursuing "a definition of being human without a specification of its content or a guarantee of its historical possibility" (Simon, 1992).

This conceptualization of teaching and learning moves away from the "sentimental and problematic assumption[s]" (Goodman, 1992, p. 133) associated with child-centered learning. Instead, it posits a more democratic classroom where the participants are given voice and "children can examine a diversity of convictions without a fear of intimidation" (Goodman, 1992, p. 157).

Such discussions, for instance, might involve interpretive discussions about artworks of the students as well as artworks in popular culture and artworks associated with high culture. Such discussions in Ms. Woolf's class began to occur in relation to the form of art as students began learning to talk to each other and critique each other's work without being overly saccharin or condemnatory. Such discussions illustrate an emerging sense of responsibility to the other in discussion and could be the grounds for building toward more difficult discussions that would recognize difference rather than suppress it. These discussions take time and the development of trust.

We do not believe that the struggle toward participatory pedagogy will be an easy one, whether it is in relation to art or to any other subject area. But we believe that this struggle is worth the energy in the same way that we believe the promotion of art as literacy at the close of the 20th century is a struggle that must be heightened if we are to develop citizens for the future who can express and interpret the world in the fullest ways possible. From the places of everyday life to digital multimedia, to the shopping bags in which we pack our lunch, to the places of the past, to the art galleries of the world, to petroglyphs and cave dwelling graphics, the visual turn (Laspina, 1998) has been upon us for some time. We must move forward to explore all of its possibilities.

NOTES

[1] See Clark (1994) for additional issues related to incorporating art into themes in the classroom. Clark also debated issues such as the advantages and disadvantages of formalism.

[2] The seven thresholds of security are the following: *noise*—the degree of tolerance for noise; *space*—the degree of tolerance for being physically close to or distant from students; *size of group*—the degree of tolerance for working with individuals, pairs, dyads, and so on; *decision making*—the degree of tolerance for student decision making; *teacher interests*—the degree to which a teacher is comfortable in letting student interests guide learning; *evaluation and standards*—the qualities teachers look for in student engagements; and *role*—the degree of explicit control the teacher exerts over the group (Courtney, as cited in Clark, 1994).

[3] Examples of such initiatives include those of Leland and Harste (1994) and Siegel (1995).

[4] See for example, Berghoff (1995), Catterall (1998a), Dudley-Marling and Murphy (1997), Gardner (1991), Harste (1994), Leland and Harste (1994), Short, Harste, and Burke (1996), Siegel (1984, 1995) and Suhor (1984).

[5] In reading research, the influence of background knowledge on the interpretation of text has been theorized and researched by numerous scholars (Anderson, 1985; Goodman, 1994; Johnston, 1984; Langer, 1984; Rosenblatt, 1994).

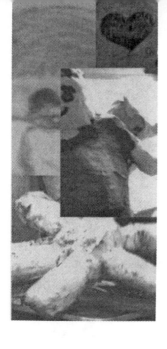

APPENDIX: METHODOLOGY NOTES

Entry

Although researchers have written about the challenges and problems in gaining access to sites (Bogdan & Biklen, 1992; Burgess, 1991; Glesne & Peshkin, 1992) and in maintaining relationships with respondents over time (Gurney, 1991), entry into RMS went smoothly. Peggy had spent time with Louise the previous year and learned that she and Louise held similar perspectives on art in the meaning making process of learners.

Louise invited Peggy to participate as an inquirer in her art room. She made the initial contacts with the principal and vice principal of the school, laying the groundwork for this study before Peggy met with them. During the first week of school, Peggy made an appointment with the vice principal and provided her with an outline of the proposed study and consent forms for student and adult respondents in the study.

Duration of Field Research

Beginning with the first week of school and continuing through the first year until May, Peggy spent two periods 1 or 2 days per week with Louise. Louise's art classes, in this first year, met for 6 weeks for a total of 12 different groups of sixth-grade students. During the first six-week period, Peggy observed Louise's teaching, her talk with students, the curriculum design, and the social dynamics of the classroom. This observation also included the artworks and critique journals of the students.

Peggy told the students that she was "a learning artist." She engaged in completing the lesson goals that the students did and shared conversations with them and Louise about her and the students' artworks. At the end of the two periods, Peggy and Louise used Louise's preparation period to reflect on the class's engagement with the lesson goals, Louise's ideas for change, the artworks produced by the students, and personal issues.

In the second year of this study, Peggy spent 3 days per week in Louise's classroom, again observing and participating in art and conversations with sixth-grade students. The school extended art classes from 6 weeks to 9 weeks. Peggy often arrived several minutes early and observed the students in the hallways, engaged in conversation with the homeroom teacher assigned to Louise's room, and talked with Louise during both the advisory period and her preparation period after the two sixth-grade classes. During this second year, Peggy also talked with eight groups of sixth grade students. At the end of the school year in May, Peggy discontinued her visitations to this classroom, but maintained a friendship with Louise.

Approach to Research

Wolcott (1994) identified three major modes through which qualitative researchers gather their data: "participant observation (experiencing), interviewing (enquiring), and studying materials prepared by others (examining)" (p. 10).

Participant Observation

Participant observation constituted a large part of Peggy's field work. Bogdan and Biklen (1992) defined a participant observer as "often remain[ing] detached, waiting to be looked over and hopefully accepted. As relationships develop, he or she participates more" (p. 88). Glesne and Peshkin (1992) suggested a difference between observer as participant and participant as observer, the former interacting less extensively in the setting than the latter. In the first year, Peggy perceived herself as working more as an observer–participant, but found that students nudged her into a more active role as a participant–observer.

Students invited Peggy into conversations and asked for comments on the construction of their artworks. In a way, they saw her as a teacher (as they might have most adults in a school), but her participation in the art lessons worked against the construction of her role as a teacher. If students asked her what she was doing in the class, Peggy indicated that she was trying to understand more clearly how and why they created the artworks that they did. She positioned herself at the students' tables, but removed herself at times from the conversations to record field notes and reflect on the students' process of meaning making.

As a participant–observer, Peggy engaged in the class activities and observed particular phenomena related to the study: (a) the teacher's lesson goals, (b) the teacher's talk and interaction with students as they constructed art, (c) the teacher's presentation of material in minilessons, (d) the teacher's overall curriculum for the 9 weeks and how students responded to it, (e) the students' talk and interaction with each other as they constructed art, (f) the role that the school structure played in its understanding about art as a school subject, and (g) Peggy's own talk and interaction with teacher and student respondents. Primary sources of data, besides field notes, included interviews and the examination of relevant artifacts.

Interviews

While in this role of participant–observer, Peggy engaged respondents in formal and informal interviews. Reinharz (1992) argues that interviewing provides inquirers with free interaction with informants, maximizes discovery and description, and allows inquirers to make full use of the differences among people. This method also invites informants to share their ideas, thoughts, and memories in their own words. Interviews enabled a more fulsome understanding of the attitudes of the students and teacher toward art before they engaged in the art curriculum, and the changes in these attitudes after 6 or 9 weeks.

Nearly all of the interviews might be defined as informal. For instance, questions were asked of students as they were constructing their artworks to understand their meaning making processes in relation to the particular work at hand. Occasionally, a preset list of questions was used with students. Students also were invited ask questions of Peggy, which helped to establish a more reciprocal relationship. Reinharz (1992) suggested that reciprocity is consistent "in avoiding control over others and developing a sense of connectedness with people" (p. 20). Informal interviews were conducted with seventh- and eighth-grade students to get a better sense of their evolving view of art and themselves as artists.

A tape recorder was used to record the ongoing conversations at the art tables as well as conversations with Louise. During class, Louise wore a lapel microphone while she talked and worked with students. Although the use of tape recorders may have invited more artificial than natural responses from students, it would have been impossible for Peggy to participate in art lessons and take field notes at the same time. The technology permitted transparency in terms of indicating to all that their comments were of interest in understanding art as literacy. It allowed Peggy to develop a stronger relationality with participants in the setting rather than be remote from it as would have been the case with an observer/recorder stance, and it permitted later review of taped conversations (which were transcribed).

Although it was recognized that tape recorders and the occasional writing of field notes initially might be intrusive for the students, and perhaps even for Louise (although she claimed otherwise), data collection did not begin until after Peggy had worked and talked with students as learning artists for several days and students appeared to have become accustomed to the tape recorder. For the most part, the students appeared to talk freely about how they constructed their artworks. Those who did not were encouraged to participate, but if they did not, their silence was respected.

Examination of Artifacts

Written and nonwritten data sources included items such as school documents, student artifacts, student art journals, and handouts for art class constructed by the teacher. The students' artworks were among the most important sources. Photographs were taken of the students at work, the students' artworks, the classroom itself, and other pieces of work that resided on school hallway walls. School and class documents relevant to the study, extensive field notes of class procedures, lessons and minilessons presented by Ms. Wolf, and students' written artist journals in which they reflected on their process of constructing a particular artwork in a particular medium were among the artifacts examined.

The fact that data were drawn from more than eight separate classes of sixth-grade students allowed for a greater degree of confidence in the interpretation of the classroom activities such as the teacher's role, curriculum stability and change, student patterns of interaction, and the impact of school and community ideology. This wider sphere of data collection was essential for examining the complex semiotic nature of literacy and the dynamic interplay of the teacher's practice, the students' processes of constructing meaning, and the personal and social histories that students' brought to their visual, written, and verbal texts. Furthermore, gathering data that specifically demonstrated various sign systems operating in synchronicity, as Harste (1994) argued, "offers new insights and new knowledge" (p. 1226).

Data Analysis

To distill the main units, structures, and processes of meaning making, several initial techniques were relied on to identify important categories. Ideas, concepts, and opinions that recurred, ideas or concepts that were communicated strongly, and illogical or inconsistent practices or ideas formed the basis of preliminary coding categories for data. Core categories were subdivided as necessary. Several other researchers, including Louise Woolf, the teacher, read drafts of the categories and commented on them. Insights from these commentaries form the basis for an additional revision of the interpretation of the data.

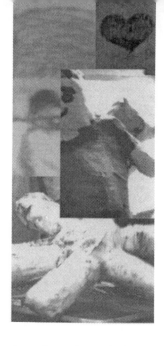

REFERENCES

American Association of University Women. (1992). *How schools short-change girls.* New York: AAUW Foundation.

Anderson, R. C. (1985). Role of the reader's schema in comprehension, learning, and memory. In H. Singer & R. B. Ruddell (Eds.), *Theoretical models and processes of reading* (3rd ed., pp. 372–384). Newark, DE: International Reading Association.

Arnstine, D. (1990). Art, aesthetics, and the pitfalls of discipline-based art education. *Educational Theory, 40* (4), 415–422.

Arnstine, D. (1995). *Democracy and the arts of schooling.* Albany, NY: SUNY Press.

Astington, J. W. (1993). *The child's discovery of the mind.* Cambridge, MA: Cambridge University Press.

Bakhtin, M. M. (1990). *Art and answerability: Early philosophical essays by M. M. Bakhtin* (M. Holquist & V. Liapunov, Eds; V. Liapunov & K. Brostrom, Trans.). Austin, TX: University of Texas Press.

Bartlett, F. C. (1932). *Remembering.* Cambridge, England: Cambridge University Press.

Barton, D., & Hamilton, M. (1997). *Local literacies: Reading and writing in one community.* London: Routledge.

Belenky, M., Clichy, B., Goldberger, N., & Tarule, J. (1986). *Women's ways of knowing: The development of self, voice, and mind.* New York: Basic Books.

Berghoff, B. (1995). *Inquiry curriculum from a semiotic perspective: First graders using multiple sign systems to learn.* Unpublished dissertation. Indiana University, Bloomington, IN.

Berland, J., Straw, W., & Tomas, D. (1996). *Theory rules: Art as theory/ theory and art.* Toronto: University of Toronto Press.

Bland, J. C. (1968). *Art of the young child: Understanding and encouraging creative growth in children three to five.* New York: Museum of Art.

Bloome, D., & Bailey, F. M. (1992). Studying language and literacy through events, particularity, and intertextuality. In R. Beach, J. L. Green, M. L. Kamil, & T. Shanahan (Eds.), *Multidisciplinary perspectives on literacy research* (pp. 181–210). Urbana, IL: National Council of Teachers of English.

Bogdan, R. C., & Biklen, S. K. (1992). *Qualitative research for education.* Boston: Allyn & Bacon.

Brittain, W. L. (1979). *Creativity, art, and the young child.* New York: Macmillan.

Britzman, D. P. (1991). *Practice makes practice: A critical study of learning to teach.* Albany, NY: SUNY Press.

Britzman, D. P. (1995). Is there a queer pedagogy? Or, stop reading straight. *Educational Theory, 45* (2), 151–165.

Britzman, D. P. (1998). *Lost subjects, contested objects: Toward a psychoanalytic inquiry of learning.* Albany, NY: SUNY Press.

Broudy, H. S. (1990). DBAE: Complaints, reminisces, and response. *Educational Theory, 40* (4), 431–435.

Brown, L. M., & Gilligan, C. (1992). *Meeting at the crossroads: Women's psychology and girls' development.* New York: Ballantine Books.

Bruner, J. (1996). *The culture of education.* Cambridge, MA: Harvard University Press.

Bullowa, M. (Ed.). (1979). *Before speech: The beginning of interpersonal communication.* Cambridge, MA: Cambridge University Press.

Burgess, R. G. (1991). Sponsors, gatekeepers, members, and friends: Access in educational settings. In W. B. Shaffir & R. A. Stebbins (Eds.), *Experiencing fieldwork: An inside view of qualitative research* (pp. 53–61). Newbury Park, CA: Sage.

Calkins, L. (1986). *The art of teaching writing.* Portsmouth, NH: Heinemann.

Carter, R., Goddard, A., Reah, D., Sanger, K., & Bowering, M. (1997). *Working with texts: A core book for language analysis.* London: Routledge.

Catterall, J. S. (1998a). *Involvement in the arts and success in secondary school.* Monograph V. 1, No. 9. Washington, DC: Americans for the Arts.

Catterall, J. S. (1998b). Does experience in the arts boost academic achievement? A response to Eisner. *Art Education, 51*(6), 6–11.

Chong, S. (1998). Policies affecting arts education: The heart of the matter. *Arts Education Policy Review, 99* (3), 22–26.

Christian-Smith, L. (1990). *Becoming a woman through romance.* New York: Routledge.

Clark, R. (1994). *Art education: A Canadian perspective.* Toronto: Ontario Society for Education through Art.

Cohen, E. P. & Gainer, E. S. (1995). *Art: Another language for learning* (3rd ed.). Portsmouth, NH: Heinemann.

Collins, G. (1995). Art education as a negative example of gender-enriching curriculum. In J. Gaskell & J. Willinsky (Eds.), *Gender in/forms curriculum: From enrichment to transformation* (pp. 43–58). New York: Teachers College Press.

Collins, R., & Sandell, R. (1984). *Women, art, and education.* Reston, VA: National Art Education Association.

Crystal, D. (1987). *The Cambridge encyclopedia of language.* Cambridge, England: Cambridge University Press.

Davilla, D. E., & Koenig, S. M. (1998). Bringing the Reggio concept to American educators. *Art Education, 51*(6), 18–24.

Davis, S. (1991). *Definitions of art.* Ithaca, NY: Cornell University Press.

Dewey, J. (1911). Is co-education injurious to girls? *Ladies Home Journal, 28*, 22 & 60–61.

Dewey, J. (1934). *Art as experience.* New York: Capricorn Books.

Dewey, J. (1938). *Education and experience.* New York: Collier Books.

Diamond, S. (1990). *Spiritual warfare: The politics of the Christian right.* New York: Black Rose Books.

Dudley-Marling, C., & Murphy, S. (1997). Editors' pages. *Language Arts, 74*, 314–315.

Efland, A. D. (1990). *A history of art education: Intellectual and social currents in teaching the visual arts.* New York: Teachers College Press.

Eisner, E. (1990). Discipline-based art education: Conceptions and misconceptions. *Educational Theory, 40*(4), 423–430.

Eisner, E. W. (1995). Why the arts are marginalized in our schools: One more time. *On Common Ground, 5,* 9.

Eisner, E. (1997). The state of art education today and some potential remedies: A report to the national endowment for the arts. *Art Education, 50* (1), 27–72.

Fausto-Sterling, A. (1985). *Myths of gender: Biological theories about women and men.* New York: Basic Books.

Fehr, D. (1994). Promise and paradox: Art education in the postmodern arena. *Studies in Art Education, 35* (4), 209–217.

Ferguson, R. (1990). Introduction: Invisible center. In R. Ferguson, M. Gever, T. T. Minh-ha, & C. West (Eds.), *Out there: Marginalization and contemporary cultures* (pp. 9–14). New York: New Museum of Contemporary Art.

Ferreiro, E., & Teberosky, A. (1982). *Literacy before schooling.* Portsmouth, NH: Heinemann.

Fineberg, J. (1997). *The innocent eye: Children's art and the modern artist.* Princeton: Princeton University Press.

Freedman, K. (1994). Interpreting gender and visual culture in art classrooms. *Studies in Art Education, 35*(3), 157–170.

Gallas, K. (1991). Art as epistemology: Enabling children to know what they know. *Harvard Educational Review, 61*(1), 19–31.

Garb, T. (1993). The forbidden gaze: Women artists and the male nude in late nineteenth-century France. In K. Adler & M. Pointon (Eds.), *The body imaged: The human form and visual culture since the renaissance* (pp. 33–42). Cambridge, MA: Cambridge University Press.

Gardner, H. (1991). *The unschooled mind: How children think and how schools should teach.* New York: Basic Books.

Geller, C. (1999). Let's keep language in language arts classrooms. *English Journal, 88*(3), 12–13.

Gilbert, P., & Taylor, S. (1991). *Fashioning the feminine: Girls, popular culture, and schooling.* Sydney: Allen & Unwin.

Gilligan, C. (1990). Teaching Shakespeare's sister. In C. Gilligan, N. Lyons, & T. Hanmer (Eds.), *Making connections: The relational worlds of adolescent girls at Emma Willard School* (pp. 6–29). New York: Troy.

Glesne, C., & Peshkin, A. (1992). *Becoming qualitative researchers: An introduction.* White Plains, NY: Longman.

Golomb, C. (1989). Sculpture: The development of representational concepts in a three-dimensional medium. In D. J. Hargreaves (Ed.), *Children and art* (pp. 105–118). Philadelphia: Open University Press.

Golomb, C. (1992). *The child's creation of a pictorial world.* Berkeley, CA: University of California Press.

Goodenough, F. L. (1926). *Measurement of intelligence by drawings.* New York: Harcourt, Brace, & World.

Goodman, J. (1992). *Elementary schooling for critical democracy.* New York: SUNY Press.

Goodman, K. S. (1994). Reading, writing, and written texts: A transactional sociopsycho-linguistic view. In R. B. Ruddell, M. R. Ruddell, & H. Singer (Eds.), *Theoretical models and processes of reading* (pp. 1093–1130). Newark, DE: International Reading Association.

Goodman, Y. M. (Ed.). (1990). *How children construct literacy: Piagetian perspectives.* Newark, DE: International Reading Association.

Green, A. (1986). *On private madness.* Madison, WI: International Universities Press.

Greene, M. (1978). *Landscapes of learning.* New York: Teachers College Press.

Greene, M. (1995). *Releasing the imagination.* San Francisco: Jossey-Bass.

Greer, W. D. (1993). Developments in discipline-based art education (DBAE): From art education toward arts education. *Studies in Art Education, 34* (2), 91–101.

Gurney, J. N. (1991). Female researchers in male-dominated settings: Implications for short-term versus long-term research. In W. B. Shaffir & R. A. Stebbing (Eds.), *Experiencing fieldwork: An inside view of qualitative research* (pp. 53–61). Newbury Park, CA: Sage.

Hall, E. T. (1976). *Beyond culture.* New York: Anchor/Doubleday.

Halliday, M. A. K. (1978). *Language as social semiotic: The social interpretation of language and meaning.* London: Edward Arnold.

Halliday, M. A. K., & Hasan, R. (1989). *Language, context, and text: Aspects of language in a social-semiotic perspective.* London: Oxford University Press.

Harste, J. C. (1994). Literacy as curricular conversations about knowledge, inquiry, and morality. In R. B. Ruddell, M. R. Ruddell, & H. Singer (Eds.), *Theoretical models and processes of reading* (pp. 1221–1242). Newark, DE: International Reading Association.

Harste, J. C., Short, K. G., & Burke, C. (1988). *Creating classrooms for authors: The reading-writing connection.* Portsmouth, NH: Heinemann.

Harste, J. C., & Vasquez, V. (1998). The work we do: Journal as audit trail. *Language Arts, 75*(4), 266–276.

Harste, J. C., Woodward, V. A., & Burke, C. L. (1984). *Language stories and literacy lessons.* Portsmouth, NH: Heinemann.

Hawkes, T. (1977). *Structuralism and semiotics*. Berkeley, CA: University of California Press.

Henneberger, M. (1998, August 9). Ralph Reed is his cross to bear. *New York Times*, Section 6, pp. 24–27.

Hildredth, G. (1941). *The child mind in evolution: A study of developmental sequences in drawing*. New York: King's Crown Press.

Hubbard, R. (1989). *Authors of pictures, draughtsmen of words*. Portsmouth, NH: Heinemann.

Jagodzinski, J. (1997). White k(night) to the rescue: Sir Arthur defends the colors of the Getty. *Studies in Art Education, 39*(1), 92–94.

Johnston, P. (1984). Prior knowledge and reading comprehension. *Reading Research Quarterly, 19,* 219–239.

Kantrowitz, B. & Kalb, C. (1998). Boys will be boys. *Newsweek, 131*(19), 54–60.

Kellogg, R., & O'Dell, S. (1967). *The psychology of children's art*. New York: CRM-Random House.

Kress, G. (1997). *Before writing*. New York: Routledge.

Kress, G., & van Leeuwen, T. (1996). *Reading images: The grammar of visual design*. London: Routledge.

Lakoff, R. T. (1990). *Talking power: The politics of language*. New York: Basic Books.

Langer, J. (1984). Examining background knowledge and text comprehension. *Reading Research Quarterly, 19*(4), 468–481.

Langer, S. K. (1957). *Philosophy in a new key: A study in the symbolism of reason, rite, and art* (3rd. ed.). Cambridge, MA: Harvard University Press.

Laspina, J. A. (1998). *The visual turn and the transformation of the textbook*. Mahwah, NJ: Lawrence Erlbaum Associates.

Lees, H. (1998). Turbulent waves: The high-speed transformation of arts education in New Zealand. *Arts Education Policy Review, 99*(3), 16–21.

Leland, C., & Harste, J. C. (1994). Multiple ways of knowing: Curriculum in a new key. *Language Arts, 71*(5), 337–345.

Lindfors, J. W. (1980). *Children's language and learning*. Englewood Cliffs, NJ: Prentice-Hall.

Lindstrom, M. (1957). *Children's art: A study of normal development in children's modes of visualization*. Berkeley, CA: University of California Press.

The Los Angeles Riots (1992). Available: *http://www.usc.edu/isd/archives/la/la_riot.html*

Lowenfeld, V., & Brittain, W.L. (1982). *Creative and mental growth* (6th Ed.). New York: Macmillan.

MacGregor, R. N. (1997). Editorial: The evolution of discipline-based art education. *Visual Arts Research, 23*(2), 1–3.

McMurtie, D. C. (1989). *The book: The story of printing and bookmaking.* New York: Dorset Press.

McNeal, J. (1997). DBAE in an Arctic fine arts program for indigenous Canadian college students. *Visual Arts Research, 23*(2), 71–82.

Miedzian, M. (1991). *Boys will be boys: Breaking the link between masculinity and violence.* New York: Doubleday Dell.

Milroy, J., & Milroy, L. (1991). *Authority in language: Investigating language prescription and standardisation* (2nd ed.). London: Routledge.

Mimms, S. K., & Lankford, E. L. (1995). Time, money, and the new art education: A nationwide investigation. *Studies in Art Education, 36*(2), 84–95.

Mittler, G., & Ragans, R. (1992). *Exploring art.* Columbus, OH: Glencoe.

Moxey, K. (1994). *The practice of theory: Poststructuralism, cultural politics, and art history.* London: Cornell University Press.

Murphy, S. (1995). *Celebrating communities: From wishes to actualities.* Paper presented at the Sixth Annual International Whole Language Umbrella Conference, July, 1995, Windsor, ON.

Murphy, S., *with* Shannon, P., Johnston, P., & Hansen, J. (1998). *Fragile evidence: A critique of reading assessment.* Mahwah, NJ: Lawrence Erlbaum Associates.

Murray, D. (1982). *Learning by teaching.* Portsmouth, NH: Boynton/Cook.

NCTE Elementary Section Steering Committee. (1996). Exploring language arts standards within a cycle of learning. *Language Arts, 73*(1), 10–13.

NCTE/IRA. (1996). *Standards for the English language arts.* Urbana, IL: National Council of Teachers of English; Newark, DE: International Reading Association.

Nespor, J. (1997). *Tangled up in school: Politics, space, bodies, and signs in the educational process.* Mahwah, NJ: Lawrence Erlbaum Associates.

O'Harrow, R. (1995, November 5). Wrangling about reading. *Washington Post-Educational Review,* pp. 10, 19.

Orner, M. B. (1992). *Teaching otherwise: Feminism, pedagogy, and the politics of difference.* Unpublished dissertation. University of Wisconsin-Madison, Madison, WI.

Pagano, J. (1990). *Exiles and communities: Teaching in the patriarchal wilderness*. Albany, New York: SUNY Press.

Paine, S. (Ed.). (1981). *Six children draw*. London: Academic Press.

Paley, N. (1995). *Finding art's place: Experiments in contemporary education and culture*. London: Routledge.

Piper, M. (1994). *Reviving Ophelia: Saving the selves of adolescent girls*. New York: Ballantine Books.

Pontecorvo, C., Orsolini, M., Burge, B., & Resnick, L.B. (Eds.). (1996). *Children's early text construction*. Hillsdale, NJ: Lawrence Erlbaum Associates.

Rayner, K., & Posnansky, C. (1978). Stages of processing in word identification. *Journal of Experimental Psychology: General, 107*, 64–80.

Reinharz, S. (1992). *Feminist methods in social research*. New York: Oxford University Press.

Rollins, T., & K.O.S. (1995). Conversation with Tim Rollins and K.O.S. In N. Paley (Ed.), *Finding art's place: Experiments in contemporary education and culture* (pp. 42–51). London: Routledge.

Rosenblatt, L. (1938). *Literature as exploration*. New York: The Modern Language Association of America.

Rosenblatt, L. (1994). *The reader, the text, the poem*. Carbondale, IL: Southern Illinois University Press.

Sadker, M., & Sadker, D. (1994). *Failing at fairness: How our schools cheat girls*. New York: Simon & Schuster.

Schiller, M. (1995). Reggio Emilia: A focus on emergent curriculum and art. *Art Education, 48*(3), 45–50.

Short, K. G., Harste, J. C., & Burke, C. (1996). *Creating classrooms for authors and inquirers*. Portsmouth, NH: Heinemann.

Siegel, M. G. (1984). *Reading as signification*. Unpublished dissertation. Indiana University, Bloomington, Indiana.

Siegel, M. G. (1995). More than words: The generative power of transmediation for learning. *Canadian Journal of Education, 20*(4), 455–475.

Simon, R. (1992). *Teaching against the grain: Texts for a pedagogy of possibility*. New York: Bergin & Garvey.

Simpson, P. (1993). *Language, ideology, and point of view*. London: Routledge.

Spodek, B., & Saracho, O. N. (Eds.). (1993). *Language and literacy in early childhood education. Yearbook in early childhood education, Vol. 4*. New York: Teachers College Press.

Staniszewski, M. A. (1995). *Believing is seeing: Creating the culture of art.* New York: Penguin.

Steiner, W. (1995). *The scandal of pleasure: Art in an age of fundamentalism.* Chicago: University of Chicago Press.

Steward, E. P. (1995). *Beginning writers in the zone of proximal development.* Hillsdale, NJ: Lawrence Erlbaum Associates.

Stroop, J. R. (1935). Studies of interference in serial verbal reactions. *Journal of Experimental Psychology, 18,* 643–662.

Suhor, C. (1984). Towards a semiotics-based curriculum. *Journal of Curriculum Studies, 16,* 247–257.

Tannen, D. (1989). *Talking voices: Repetition, dialogue, and imagery in conversational discourse.* New York: Cambridge University Press.

Teale, W. H., & Sulzby, E. (Eds.). (1986). *Emergent literacy: Writing and reading.* Norwood, NJ: Ablex.

Temple, C. A., Temple, R. G., & Burris, N. A. (1982). *The beginning of writing.* Boston: Allyn & Bacon.

Thomas, A., & Chess, S. (1977). *Temperament and development.* New York: Brunner/Mazel.

Thompson, J.M. (Ed.) (1990). *Twentieth century theories of art.* Ottawa, Canada: Carleton University Press.

Thorne, B. (1993). *Gender play: Girls and boys in school.* New Brunswick, NJ: Rutgers University Press.

Tickle, L. (1996a). Art, art education, and the next century. In L. Tickle (Ed.), *Understanding art in primary schools: Cases from teachers' research* (pp. 16–27). London: Routledge.

Tickle, L. (1996b). Visual art and teacher research in primary schools. In L. Tickle (Ed.), *Understanding art in primary schools: Cases from teachers' research* (pp.1–15). London: Routledge.

Vasta, R. (Ed.). (1982). *Strategies and techniques of child study.* Toronto: Academic Press.

Volosinov, V. (1983). *Marxism and the philosophy of language* (L. Matejka & I. R. Titunik, Trans.). Cambridge, MA: Cambridge University Press.

Walkerdine, V. (1990). *Schoolgirl fictions.* New York: Verso.

White, B. E. (1978). Introduction. In B. E. White (Ed.), *Impressionism in perspective* (pp. 1–6). Englewood Cliffs, NJ: Prentice-Hall.

Wink, J. (1997). *Critical pedagogy: Notes from the real world.* New York: Longman.

Winner, E. (1982). *Invented worlds: The psychology of the arts.* Cambridge, MA: Cambridge University Press.

Winterson, J. (1995). *Art objects: Essays on ecstasy and effrontery.* Toronto: Alfred A. Knopf.

Wolcott, H. (1994). *Transforming qualitative data.* Thousand Oaks, CA: Sage.

Wolff, J. (1993). *Aesthetics and the sociology of art* (2nd ed.). Ann Arbor: University of Michigan Press.

Young, K. G. (1987). *Taleworlds and storyrealms: The phenomenology of of the narrative.* Boston: Martinus Nijhoff.

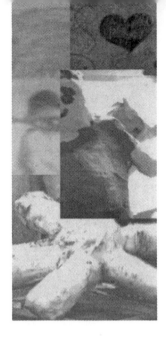

AUTHOR INDEX

SUBJECT INDEX

158   SUBJECT INDEX